Prisoners of the Tsar

East Coast Sailors Held In Russia
1800-1801

by

Rosalin Barker

On 8 November, 1800,
His Imperial Majesty, Paul the First, Tsar and Autocrat of All the Russias, member of the Second Coalition of allies against Napoleon, issued a decree that all British shipping in the Baltic ports of his Empire should be placed under an Embargo, and that the crews should be removed from on board and taken by force into the interior of Russia.

Highgate Publications (Beverley) Ltd.
1992

© Copyright Rosalin Barker 1992

British Library Cataloguing in Publication Data
Barker, Rosalin
  Prisoners of the Tsar: East Coast Sailors
  Held in Russia, 1800-01
  I. Title
  947

  ISBN 0-948929-57-x

Published by Highgate Publications (Beverley) Ltd.
24 Wylies Road, Beverley. HU17 7AP.
Telephone (0482) 866826

Printed and Typeset in 10 on 11pt Times by
Colourspec, Unit 7, Tokenspire Park,
Hull Road, Woodmansey, Beverley. HU17 0TB.
Telephone (0482) 864264

Cover Illustration:

The pioneering photographer Frank Meadow Sutcliffe spent his working life mainly in Whitby. Although most of his photographs were of people and places, he took a series of pictures of sailing ships at the end of the 19th century at the time when they were being ousted by steam. This is one of his most evocative and best-loved shots. (FMS)

Key to Caption Credits

Etty	*The Etty Family*
FMS	*The Sutcliffe Gallery, in association with Whitby Literary and Philosophical Society*
IAB	*Ian A. Barker*
IP	*Mrs. I. Plumb*
RB	*Rosalin Barker, personal collection*
TE	Whitby Prints, *T. E. English*
WLP	*Whitby Literary and Philosophical Society*

ACKNOWLEDGEMENTS

I have, over the past two years, received so much help and encouragement that it is difficult to know where to begin the acknowledgements. Perhaps the first thanks ought to go to Mr. John Bourne and Mr. Bartley Feeney who were instrumental in bringing Thomas Etty and his Journal to my attention, and to Mrs. Iris Plumb, its owner, for allowing me to work on it. I must then thank most sincerely the Local Population Studies Society for the generous Scholarship I was given to enable me to undertake the travel involved in the research.

The research has involved many repositories of documents and libraries, to all of which I owe gratitude, but particularly to the staff of the Public Record Office, especially at Kew; to the staff of the Guildhall Library and the City of London Record Office; to Mr. D. Vasey and staff of the Scottish Record Office, and to the staff of the National Library for Scotland; to the Archivists of West Yorkshire Archives at Leeds, and North Yorkshire County Record Office; to those at York City Archives and at the Borthwick Institute of Historical Research; to the Curator at York City Art Gallery, and the staff of York Central Library, of the Local Studies Library at Hull Central Library and of Newcastle Central Library. Above all, I am grateful to my friends and colleagues at Whitby Museum.

During the last two years I have spoken to many groups about the search for Thomas Etty and his companions in misery, and I have been glad of both searching questions and of snippets of information, and of encouragement to continue the search.

Colleagues and friends, particularly Peter Frank of the University of Essex, and Gordon Humphreys of the University of Leeds, have helped with the Russian aspects, finding me maps of Russia and putting me in touch with Estonian and Lithuanian academics. Donald Woodward and Barbara English of the University of Hull gave me advice and encouragement over finding of English sources for the period, as did Mr. D. J. Lyon of the National Maritime Museum. My own extra-mural students gathered little bits of information for me as they followed their own researches.

I am grateful to those who have helped me with illustrations, particularly Whitby Literary and Philosophical Society, the Sutcliffe Gallery, John Tindale, Mr. W. T. Brown of Sandsend, and Hugh and Charles English, as well as to Messrs Thomas Etty, senior and junior, both resident in the Netherlands, for sharing with me so much of their family's history, and for permission to use the picture of the earlier Thomas painted by his brother William. The list can never be exhaustive; however, I must save my principal thanks for my family, who have been so tremendously supportive of me and tolerant of my papers and computer, and absences and abstractions, while I did the research and wrote the book.

Lastly I owe gratitude to Thomas Etty, 1780-1854, whose careful preservation of his little book has made this possible.

Rosalin Barker

Dedication
For my Family

Thomas Etty, aged 31, around the time of the death of his first wife. This was painted by his brother, William, later Royal Academician, and is one of a series of portraits of his family. The original is in the Netherlands, in the care of the Etty family. (Etty)

The Opal *in Whitby; she is a fine collier brig. The tall, rather angular building to the right of her is Simpson and Chapman's Bank. From the roof the partners could contemplate their large investments in Whitby, and both families were associated with the Russia Company. (FMS)*

CHAPTER 1

Thomas Etty was born in Feasegate, in the parish of All Saints, Pavement, with Little St Peter's, in the City of York, on 9 April, 1780. He was the son of Esther and Matthew Etty. Esther Calverley had married Matthew Etty, one of her family's tenants, against their wishes, and they had been forced to leave their home community of Hayton, in the East Riding, and try their fortune in York in Matthew's trade of miller, to which was added the skill of ginger-bread making at which they became well-known. The surviving members of their numerous family were Walter, who became a gold and silver lace and epaulette merchant, with his uncle, Thomas Bodley, in London; John, who became a miller and property owner in York; Thomas; Charles, who, like Thomas, was apprenticed to the sea, but who became a sugar manufacturer in Java; and the youngest, William, who became an esteemed painter after an apprenticeship in the printing trade in Hull.

At the age of 13, Thomas was sent to Whitby to be apprenticed to John Chapman, shipowner, a member of a large and important family of shipowners, merchants and bankers in Whitby. As an apprentice or servant, he worked on board a ship, in the care of one of Chapman's masters, first Aaron Chapman, then Jonathan Barker, and in winter would be fed, boarded and educated at Chapman's expense. It was thus that he learnt the required skills of keeping a ship's log and in accounts, which he was to keep with such desperate accuracy during his long imprisonment. Thomas went to sea as a 'servant' on John Chapman's ship the *Jane*, serving there until she was lost, cause unrecorded, in 1796.

Thomas must by then have been well-grown and out of his 'time', for he is listed, in 1797, among the crew of another of John Chapman's ships, the *William and Mary*, as a seaman, when he would have been 17 years old.

The next year his youngest brother, William, was apprenticed as a printer to Mr. William Peck, editor of the *Hull Packet*, in Scale Lane, Hull, and William's biographer, Alexander Gilchrist, recorded that about this time Thomas, on leave from the whale fishery, gave the small William his first paintbox. At the end of his apprenticeship in Hull, William, already a skilled artist, set off for London, where his elder brother, Walter, supported him while he attended the Royal Academy and progressed in his career. Thomas' kindness was not forgotten, and was reciprocated later when Thomas' own fortunes were at a low ebb.

1

Ship Jane's Muster Roll - 1793, 1794, 1795 & 1796

Name of Crewman	Post	Date	Date	Mths/Days
Aaron Chapman	Master	15/3/1793	18/11/1793	08.03
Jonathan Barker	Mate &	ditto	ditto	08.03
	Master	18/11/1793	12/11/1796 (ship lost)	35.24
Robt Braithwaite	Carpenter	15/3/1793	ditto	43.27
William Day	2nd. Mate & Mate	ditto	ditto	43.27
William Williams	2nd. Mate	ditto	ditto	43.27
John Hudson	Boatswain	ditto	ditto	43.27
John Jessels	Seaman	ditto	ditto	43.27
Hugh Marwick	ditto	ditto	ditto	43.27
Alexander Steele	ditto	ditto	ditto	43.27
John Wilson	ditto	ditto	ditto	43.27
William Grant	ditto	ditto	ditto	43.27
George Burnham	ditto	ditto	ditto	43.27
Thomas Howard	ditto	ditto	ditto	43.27
Abraham Platt	ditto	ditto	ditto	43.27
William Trattles	Servant	ditto	ditto	43.27
Henry Wood	ditto	ditto	ditto	43.27
Robert Etty	ditto	ditto	ditto	43.27
Thomas Etty	ditto	ditto	ditto	43.27

At 6d. per Month 754 months, 12 days,
£18:17:2 Paid July, 1797

Ship Jane's Muster Roll from 15 March, 1793, to 12 November, 1796, the day she was lost.

   While William was still in Hull, well into his time with Mr. Peck, he would have had the unenviable task of helping to set in type the accounts of the imprisonment of the men caught in the embargo, among them his kindhearted brother Tom. By 1800 Thomas was apparently, although his name does not appear on the ship's muster roll, on board the *George*, sailing in the Baltic trade, carrying timber and other naval stores badly needed for the war against the French, to the shipyards of the Thames. It was from the *George* that he had the greatest of all his adventures, and possibly the last, and from the *George* that he left his account of the ordeal of the captured British seamen.

CHAPTER 2

The port of Whitby was at the height of its economic strength in 1800, the seventh port in Britain, despite its isolated position cut off from the rest of England by the North York Moors. It was a subsidiary – or creek – port of Newcastle upon Tyne, with whom it had had for the many years of its growing prosperity a very uneasy relationship. Whitby was engaged in ship-building, ship-owning and ship-manning. Its ships carried coal from the north-eastern coalfields to London, and fished the Greenland whale in the Arctic, as well as more humble cod, haddock and herring in the North Sea. It provided about 20% of the ships and men engaged in the Baltic trade. The proportion of Whitby ships caught up in the Baltic Incident was exactly that: 45 out of 209. Whitby ships were in great demand for the Navy as transports, because of their good design, large capacity and great strength, and their seamen were favoured as naval transport crews. The *George* herself was, at a later date, one such ship.

The *George* was built in 1796 by one of Whitby's best-known yards, that of George and Nathaniel Langborne, and was owned by a third member of the same family, William Langborne. He was her managing owner, or ship's husband, although he is unlikely to have owned her outright. There would most likely have been 64 shares in the vessel, and the other owners may have had investments in several ships. Recent research shows that most investors in Whitby ships were from within the community, which was surprisingly wealthy for such a small place, a town of some 9-10,000 inhabitants.

The ship was measured at 366 tons for her registration, and probably carried about 600 tons of cargo. She was 104 feet long, and 29 feet at her beam. As the term *ship* indicates, she was three-masted and square-rigged. Her master from her building to 1816 when he retired from the sea was Thomas Coverdale, one of three brothers, all master mariners. When he died in 1823, aged about 72, he left his navigation instruments to his brothers, for he seems to have had no other family. He was just under 50 when he was captured, a respected member of the community, a good friend of the Langbornes. The ship's muster shows a crew of 13, but it is likely that there were at least 15 aboard, including Mates, carpenter and cook, with five servants or apprentices. Seafaring was a young man's trade, but there were several mature men among the crew, although some of the servants may have been as young as 13 or even less. It is not known how many survived in Russia, for in the scramble at Riga to crew the ships and make up for lost time there would be many changes of crew.

As in all ports trading in and out of the Thames, the shipowners of Whitby had to pay, probably reluctantly, the Seamen's Sixpence, towards the upkeep of Greenwich Hospital. This was a levy of 6d. for every month at sea for every member of the crew. There is evidence that the crews were under-recorded, as merchant seamen objected to paying for the upkeep of a naval institution for which they were ineligible, although the rules had been emended to make Greenwich available to mercantile seamen injured in war, and to allow part of the levy to be allocated to the various charitable Seamen's Hospitals in the 'outports'. Whitby had one such hospital, founded in 1675. Not only have many of the official returns for this levy survived for Whitby, but in the Whitby Seamen's Hospital there were recently discovered the original schedules from which these returns were normally made.

The returns consist of muster rolls for the vessels, giving the name, post on board and voyage history of each crew member. There are few long runs of these returns left, and the best collections are in the Yorkshire area.

SEAMEN'S HOSPITAL HOUSES.

WHITBY,

JANUARY, 1905.

The Committee of the above have learnt with regret that there has been a considerable amount of bad language used by some of the tenants when under the influence of drink, and THIS IS TO GIVE NOTICE that any of the tenants found guilty of being under the influence of drink or using bad language, will immediately receive notice to quit and deliver up possession of the house they occupy.

By Order of

THE COMMITTEE.

A stern reminder that charity depended on the good behaviour of the recipients. (WLP)

NOTICE.

A Meeting of the Trustees

OF THE

SEAMEN'S FUND,

WILL BE HELD

At the SEAMEN'S HOUSE,

ON MONDAY,

At Half-past TEN o'clock in the Forenoon,

TO DISPOSE OF

VACANT HOUSE

All Applicants are requested to attend.

Whitby,   188 .

BY ORDER,

John Hudson, Printer Bookbinder, Stationer, &c., Flowergate, Whitby.

Whitby's Seamen's Hospital was established in 1675 and in 1754 was added to the list of those which might benefit from the Seamen's Sixpence. As a result, a long series of Muster Rolls has survived. The Hospital still functions; the house came vacant in the 1880s. (WLP)

CHAPTER 3

The *George* of Whitby was in Bulroye (Bolderaja), a port in present-day Latvia, about ten kilometres nearer the sea than the capital, Riga, when the trouble began. Although Whitby ships brought some shipbuilding supplies to her own busy yards, the bulk of her fleet carried such stores to the Thames and Portsmouth for the Royal Navy. The Baltic was the prime source of timber for masts and spars, hemp, flax and tar for ship-building. The need for these was exacerbated by the long duration of the wars with France. Indeed, the embargo took place during the War of the Second Coalition, 1798-1802. So desperate was the demand that newspapers of the time recorded the speed with which British ships could sail from the Thames to St Petersburg, quoting 14 days as a remarkable effort by one ship. The normal round trip was about two months, with some three to five voyages per annum the usual rate.

The Baltic trade was controlled by the Russia Company, which had come into being in 1553 as the Muscovy Company, seeking to control, through monopoly, all trade with the growing empire of Ivan IV (The Terrible). It was based in the City of London, where its affairs were conducted by a President and a Court of Assistants. Its Minute Books and accounts are an invaluable source for the Baltic trade, and for the history of merchant shipping. As the Russian Empire grew so the trading base of the Company expanded. Its Charter was confirmed in 1566 by Queen Elizabeth and in 1586 it was reconstructed as the Russia Company. In 1597 its power over trade in eastern Europe increased when the great Hanseatic League was forced by Queen Elizabeth to close its London headquarters, the Stillyard. Some of the ports with which it eventually traded were themselves members of the Hanseatic League.

The Company restricted all trade between England and much of Eastern Europe to those merchants and shipowners who were its Members. However, the Navigation Acts and Ordinances of the mid-17th century restricted trade with the growing English colonies to English shipping, giving English merchants exclusive access to a growing market, even to the exclusion of the Scots, and the importance of English trade with Russia declined to the point where the Russia Company was forced to open trading access to Russia to anyone who would pay the £5 membership fee which made him a Freeman. Much of the British income of the Company came from these fees, from 'mulcts', or fines, for trading without membership, and from dues collected at all ports round the country which traded with Russia.

As Whitby's ship-building and ship-owning expanded, and as the Russian Empire grew to take in the Baltic states, from which came many of the raw materials for ship-building, agents were appointed in the port, and returns of dues were made annually. A list of the Freemen (and women – there were some formidable women among the shipowners, and even banking partners, of Whitby at the time) from Whitby represents most of the shipping interest in the town. Nevertheless, compared with other ports such as Hull, the amount of dues collected by Thomas Robinson, the Deputy Customer and Company Agent for imports into the town, was often small. Whitby's large shipping fleet, which carried one fifth of all the cargo between the Baltic and Great Britain, was a service industry, touching its home port only to be repaired or to lie up during the winter. Francis Gibson, Customer, and Commanding Officer of the Militia in Whitby, wrote of the high value of the Baltic fishing fleet laid up in Whitby during the winter, when he drew up his map of suggested defences for the town. Even so, the 'lay-ups' were often in London, to ensure a quick departure as soon as the ice which beset the Baltic, especially the Gulf of Riga, was known to be easing. The Baltic voyages are often revealed in the Muster Rolls only by the dates at which they took place, for the season was shorter than the coal-trading season, though longer than that of the whale-fishery. The *William and Mary*, which sailed initially from London, and later touched Portsmouth, where Thomas Etty joined her crew, recorded the distinctive dates of a Baltic trader.

The cargo carried by Whitby ships was mainly for the naval shipyards. The Navy Board, which controlled the purchase of all naval stores, and which was responsible for the building and repair of ships, and therefore heavily involved in the Baltic trade and this incident, was founded only eight years before the Muscovy Company.

During the 18th century the rôle of the Russia Company, as far as HM Government was concerned, had become advisory. It acted very largely on behalf of those important mercantile Counting Houses which traded most extensively with Russia, and whose members made up the 'Factories' in the various cities. Factories in this instance had nothing to do with manufacturing, being simply loose organisations of merchants engaged in a particular enterprise. Those Houses tended to have members permanently resident '*this*' or '*that side the water*', as the Minutes of the Court of Assistants of the Company frequently say. The Government tended to employ leading merchants as Consuls in Russia, and it was in that capacity, as well as in their normal trading rôle, that the firm of Walter Shairp and Company of London found itself embroiled in the events of 1800-1801. Stephen Shairp was HM Consul-General, and his brother Alexander was the Vice-Consul.

Most of the trade with the Baltic ports of Russia passed through Cronstadt, the fortress port for St. Petersburg, and Riga. Reval, now Tallinn, in Estonia, was a naval base, as was Cronstadt, but Wyborg on the Gulf of Finland, and Narva in Estonia were smaller trading ports. The Gulf of Riga, between Riga

Ship William and Mary's Muster Roll, 1797

Names	Post	Date entered	Date discharged	Months-Days served
George Snowdon	Master	8/5/97	18/12/97	07/10
Thomas Richardson	Mate	ditto	ditto	07/10
James Neil	Carpenter	ditto	ditto	07/10
John Medcalfe	Servant	ditto	ditto	07/10
William Peart	Servant	ditto	ditto	07/10
Richard Burton	Servant	ditto	ditto	07/10
Samuel Johnson	Servant	ditto	ditto	07/10
Thomas English	Cook	ditto	19/8/97	03/11
Thomas Forrest	2nd. Mate	ditto	ditto	03/11
Richard Hempson	Seaman	ditto	ditto	03/11
Nicholas Robinson	Seaman	ditto	ditto	03/11
Richard Cummins	Seaman	ditto	ditto	03/11
James Brown	Seaman	ditto	ditto	03/11
Hans Henderson	Seaman	ditto	ditto	03/11
William Turnbull	Seaman	ditto	ditto	03/11
John Marlowe	Cook	9/9/1797	18/12/1797	03/09
Robert Gathercole	2nd. Mate	ditto	ditto	03/09
Thomas Etty	Seaman	ditto	ditto	03/09
John Jones	Seaman	ditto	ditto	03/09
James Wilson	Seaman	ditto	ditto	03/09
Jud Christopher Jacob	Seaman	ditto	ditto	03/09
Peter Thompson	Seaman	ditto	ditto	03/09
John Nicholson	Seaman	ditto	ditto	03/09

At 6d. per Month, 104 months, 20 days
£2:12:0 Paid 9 February, 1798

and Reval, froze for some four months of most years, so that trade was normally at a standstill between the beginning of December and the middle of May, and the British Baltic fleet was either laid up for repairs, or slipping a coal voyage into its 'free' time to earn extra money. The shipowners and masters of Whitby were great opportunists.

Riga, the port with which the *George* was trading, was in Latvia, annexed to Russia during the reign of Catherine the Great. It was German speaking, and an ancient Hanseatic city, standing near the mouth of the Western River Dvina. Bulroye (Bolderaja) much nearer the sea, was an outlying member of the port.

The Russians had very few merchant ships of their own, and there was some disquiet among the Court in Russia at the end of the 18th century that this enormous trade carried in foreign vessels was actually to Russia's disadvantage. The extent of the trade carried through Riga is shown by Stephen Shairp's detailed analysis of the shipments at the end of the 18th century.

There were other problems and the surviving voyage accounts of Whitby ships engaged in the Baltic trade show a disproportionate amount of damage to vessels. Sea conditions were dangerous, and ports at times chaotic, with a high risk of collision damage. Occasionally ships which were normally engaged in the coal trade would venture to the Baltic in search of greater earnings, which did indeed accrue, but at a cost in repairs that seems to have discouraged the more cautious owners. Others made an exclusive speciality of the trade, taking advantage of the opportunity to buy cheaply spare canvas, rope and spars for the ship at the same time. Much of the import was iron, of a higher quality than was readily available in England.

There was also disquiet on the British side at the quality of some of the goods, particularly of the baled goods like hemp, which often concealed both poor materials and either short weight or volume. Stamp duty which had been imposed by the Russians on the financial bonds which transferred the cost from buyer to seller made for frustration, particularly over smaller cargoes. The Scots especially, for whom the Union of Parliaments in 1707 had opened up all the trading opportunities hitherto denied them by the Navigation Acts, were beginning to find that dealing with the Russians was very trying, particularly after the accession of Paul I in 1796. There were additional pressures after the commencement of the war with France, in the form of levies designed to cover the costs of convoys to protect British shipping from French naval vessels and privateers, both of which patrolled the North Sea.

John Chapman, shipowner, banker and Freeman of the Russia Company, on whose ships, William and Mary *and* Jane, *Thomas Etty served his time as a servant. (WLP)*

The Alert, *built in 1802 by George and Nathaniel Langborne, who built the* George, *and whose brother William was Thomas Coverdale's 'good friend', and owner of the* George. *At the time when Sutcliffe photographed the* Alert *she was eighty years old, and had been converted from a sloop to a top-sailed schooner. She survived several strandings during her long life. (FMS)*

Some of the timber went into the construction of wharves rather than of ships; these wooden wharves still run alongside the River Hull in the old harbour in Hull. Thomas Etty would have known the warehouses by the Hull.(RB)

CHAPTER 4

Catherine the Great, Empress of Russia for over 30 years, had died in 1796, and had been succeeded by her son, Paul I. The new Tsar was to prove a very unstable character indeed. Like all Tsars, he was an 'Emperor and Autocrat', and ruled without any form of elected assembly. His instability was much discussed, both in Russia, which felt it most, and in Britain, where a long letter from Stephen Shairp, Consul-General in St. Petersburg, arrived in the Foreign Office in October, 1800, commenting that never was Tsar so disliked, and that the dislike was entirely personal. Shairp described at length Paul's irrational behaviour. In the West Riding Archives in Leeds the Papers of George Canning, one of the great politicians of the age, contain a personal letter from Canning to Pitt, complaining that Paul was mad. British newspapers, both national and provincial, at the time of the crisis devoted many column inches to discussions of his state of mind. The modern tabloid newspaper's simplistic reaction to all things alien is little different from that of its 18th-century predecessor.

By 1800 Britain had been at war with France since 1793, in the wake of the French Revolution. The war had several phases, and although Britain remained at war with France for another 15 years, with only one short respite, the Peace of Amiens, 27 March, 1802, to May, 1803, the alignments of her Allies changed, and during the period of Thomas' Journal, she was involved in the *War of the Second Coalition*. This alliance was established by William Pitt the Younger in December, 1798, between Britain, Austria, Russia, Naples, Turkey and Portugal, in order to try to defeat Napoleon. At the start of the Baltic crisis Pitt was still Prime Minister, though before it was over his government fell and in February, 1801, he was succeeded by Henry Addington. Pitt's letters on political affairs to his friend George Canning, who became Foreign Secretary later in the war, are preserved in the Canning Papers.

One of the standard practices of warfare was the use of the blockade against neutral merchant shipping carrying what might be deemed to be 'military contraband'. The most obvious form of contraband was weaponry, but necessary foodstuffs and the raw materials for ship-building might be regarded as contraband by a great naval power such as Britain. Enemy merchant ships were, of course, captured where possible, or sunk. Neutral ships would be arrested, either by a Royal Naval vessel, or by a privateer carrying Letters of Marque from the Crown entitling her to stop and search neutral shipping, and taken to a British or other friendly port where the cargo would be considered by a Prize Court. That body would either allow the vessel to proceed if harmless, or else 'condemn' and confiscate it if the cargo were deemed of military use. Compensation for the market value and for damage would be paid, and the now empty vessel would proceed homewards, or even itself be deemed a prize. Not surprisingly, neutral countries with a strong mercantile seafaring tradition, such as Denmark, resented this action, for it was a serious interference with both trade and freedom. Sometimes neutral governments might, though themselves apparently politically uncommitted, accept the need on strategic grounds, while at other times their reaction would be indignant. In 1780, during the War of American Independence, Britain had imposed such a blockade, and the Northern Powers, Denmark, Sweden and Russia, formed the League of Armed Neutrality to counteract Britain's action.

Among Paul's many assumed titles was that of Grand Master of the Order of St. John, whose headquarters had been in Malta until Napoleon overran the island. British newspaper commentators failed to see how anyone who was not a Roman Catholic could have acquired such an office, but some of the Knights displaced by Napoleon actually appear to have fled to Russia. In 1798 Napoleon had captured Malta from the Knights who had administered it since the 16th century. The British, having promised to hand the island back to the Order, besieged the island, which was of enormous strategic importance, and eventually captured it in September, 1800. Paul maintained that when the Siege had started it was agreed that, when the island fell, it should be to all the Allies. When, however, it was the Union Flag alone which was hoisted over Malta, Paul took great offence, despite the fact that when Sir Home Popham, the British envoy, brought confirmation of the British promise, made when the Second Coalition was established, Paul I had refused to communicate with Popham. Other pressures, including Paul's growing admiration for Napoleon, concern about the British blockade of Europe, and a desire to re-establish the League of Armed Neutrality with Denmark and Sweden, led to a series of *ukaases* or decrees laying bans or embargoes on British trade.

An earlier embargo in August gives us an insight into the methods used. The ships caught in the Baltic ports were hauled together and anchored in the middle of the harbour, with a Russian soldier on guard on each. Guard boats were appointed to row continuously around the gathered vessels, and the Captains were enjoined to keep their crews in order. Letters from Stephen Shairp, the Consul, indicated that the Russians said that this embargo was caused by violence towards Danish shipping. They said that Royal Naval vessels had entered the Sound, the narrow passage into the Baltic between Denmark and Sweden - in fact, the naval ships were two frigates on convoy duty waiting to escort British ships across the dangerous North Sea. Shairp referred also to a ban on all transactions between Russian merchants and Britain.

The situation was further complicated by the presence of many British officers in the Russian Imperial Navy, which was in any case, as were the Russian arsenals, in a deplorable state. Good intelligence officer as he was,

Stephen Shairp had his finger on every pulse. These British officers were ejected, and some sent home, where they would doubtless have been a much-needed resource for the Royal Navy, though as it transpired later, not all left, or were allowed to leave, for Captain Bunney of Hull met some of them in Moscow, as he told his wife in one of his letters. When that first embargo was lifted in September, Stephen Shairp came home on leave; he felt that the approach of winter, by which time most shipping would have left the Baltic before it iced up, and which would have slowed down Russian life, made things stable for the moment. He made quite clear to the Foreign Office his views on the instability of both Tsar and Court. He clearly foresaw 'private vengeance' against the Tsar.

Denmark had meantime protested about the arrest of her ships, and had begun to send them in armed convoy. Convoys were, in fact, used by all sides, and there are many references in Admiralty and other sources to the use of the Royal Navy to escort fleets of merchant shipping in and out of the Baltic. Vital war supplies were particularly well-guarded. An incident in the summer of 1800, in which a Danish merchant vessel was taken to Gibraltar after a skirmish between a Royal Navy frigate and the Danish Navy escort, particularly incensed Paul. The appearance of the two British frigates in the Sound in August led him to fear that Britain was going to attack the Baltic states. This fear indicated a lack of faith in his own Navy, unless he saw the frigates as forerunners of a much greater fleet.

At the commencement of the final embargo on 8 November Riga was busy with ships loading badly-needed naval supplies. A letter from the Government purchasing agent in Riga, dated 8 November, and brought to England by a member of the St. Petersburg Factory, recorded that in October some 47 ships had been despatched back to England with timber and other goods, and that another 22 which were then loading had been caught 'in the snare'. The agent commented that part of his problem had been the late arrival in the Gulf of Riga of many of these ships because they had been held up in England on government instructions after the summer flare-up of trouble between Russia and Britain. Of these the *George* was one. The *Newcastle Chronicle* had excellent lists of the passage of ships through the Sound, a narrow waterway controlled by Denmark, and these can be compared with the lists of ships captured. Sadly, the lists of captured ships compiled in the Baltic ports are not so far to be found in Admiralty or Foreign Office records, but a copy of the list was published in the *Newcastle Chronicle*. Other local newspapers, in cities such as Hull, York, Edinburgh and Dundee, carried lists of ships belonging to their own and neighbouring ports, and, with the aid of these, and of Lloyd's Register, it has been possible to reconstruct a reasonably complete list, with names of vessels, masters, ship types and in most cases home ports.

The ports of Yorkshire suffered most from the embargo, as the list of vessels captured shows:

Source: The *Newcastle Chronicle* 24 January, 1801, from a list sent from Elsinore on 13 January, 1801;

Name of Vessel	Master	Home port
Admiral Nelson	Fullam	Bridlington
Ann	Kirton	Bridlington
Centurion	Brambles	Bridlington
Concord	Nicholson	Bridlington
Dolphin	Artley	Bridlington
John and Richard	Thompson	Bridlington
Oeconomy	Groves	Bridlington
Supply	Beveridge	Bridlington
Adventure	Hardie	Hull
Armintor	Evans	Hull
Betsey	Wood	Hull
Britannia	Allison	Hull
Catherine	Russel	Hull
Commerce	Hopper	Hull
Dwina	Sharp	Hull
Flaxton	Stephenson, William	Hull
George	McKandy	Hull
Hope	Wintringham	Hull
Houghton	Ruston	Hull
John and Sarah	Bell	Hull
Kingston	Appleton	Hull
Lord Carrington	Binnington	Hull
Lyde	Taylor	Hull
Manchester	Brown	Hull
Maria	Stark	Hull
Mary Frances	Bunney	Hull
Peggy	Edington	Hull
Ploughman	Thomson/Agar, John	Hull
Refuge	Bowser	Hull
Ruby	Hemming	Hull
Tiber	Trotter	Hull
Union	Harrow	Hull
Walker	Hardy	Hull
Williamson	Wrangham	Hull
Zephyr	Brown	Hull

Name of Vessel	Master	Home port
Albion	Fothergill	Scarborough
Edward	Hughes	Scarborough
Enterprise	Camp	Scarborough
Haddock	Harrison	Scarborough
Friends	Maxwell	Selby
Rover	Wilson	Selby
Russia Company	Robinson	Selby
Adeona	Street	Whitby
Aid	Brown	Whitby
Amalthea	Stewards	Whitby
Amity	Swales	Whitby
Ann	Allen	Whitby
Ann	Harrison	Whitby
Aquilon	Cuthbertson	Whitby
Ardent	Briggs	Whitby
Benson	Hildreth	Whitby
Betsey	Pert	Whitby
Blackett	Elliott	Whitby
Britannia	Dale	Whitby
Campion	Gibson, William	Whitby
Charles	Harland	Whitby
Commerce	Loft	Whitby
Countess of Darlington	Ramsden	Whitby
Desire	Dickinson	Whitby
Edward	Fowler	Whitby
Elizabeth	Franks	Whitby
Endeavour	Teasdale	Whitby
Friendship	Coates	Whitby
George	Coverdale, Thos	Whitby
Golden Grove	Oswald	Whitby
Grafton	Pole	Whitby
Haddock	Dunning, Constable	Whitby
Harpooner	Kneeshaw	Whitby
Herald	Waite, Robert	Whitby
Isabella	Brodrick	Whitby
Jane	Watson	Whitby
John and Mary	Hanson	Whitby
Laurel	Headley	Whitby
Mary	Hutchinson	Whitby
Mary Ann	Taylor/Reay	Whitby

Name of Vessel	Master	Home port
Navigator	Robinson	Whitby
Nelly	Pixby	Whitby
Paragon	Woodcock	Whitby
Progress	Baker/Bathe	Whitby
Progress	Lacy	Whitby
Request	Ellerby	Whitby
Rodney	Bowes	Whitby
Thaïs	Pearson, Christopher	Whitby
Triton	Garner	Whitby
William	Tully, George	Whitby
William and Mary	Brown	Whitby
Zephyr	Cowham	Whitby

209 ships were caught, with over 2,000 seamen, from the whole country, but of these, 87, or 42%, were from the Yorkshire ports; at least 1,000 Yorkshire seamen were imprisoned.

The names of the vessels reflect the normal naming practices of shipowners; however, they were to inspire witty letters to the press;

Newcastle Chronicle, 17 January, 1801

The embargo laid by Russia on the English shipping is a much more serious evil than we at first imagined. From a list of vessels it appears the Emperor has by it provided himself with *Admiral Nelson, Lord Rodney, Earl Howe,* and several others of our best Admirals. Thus supported, no wonder that he has taken from us our *Commerce,* our *Prosperity,* our *Performance, Industry* and *Resolution,* leaving us without our *Fortune, Friendship, Union, Concord, Peace, Amity* and *Hope.* He has parcelled out all *Albion,* and possessed himself of *Manchester, Bedford,* etc., and deprived us of the *Prince of Wales, Lord Carrington,* and a long train of fashionable *Nymphs, Betseys, Annes, Fannys* and *Marys.* Even the winds of heaven are not suffered to visit us, as he has seized upon *Zephyr, Boreas* etc. In this situation, we are left without *Expedition, Enterprise* and *Chance.*

[*Only* 'Peace' *and* 'Boreas' *are not on any list so far discovered but one must allow for a little journalistic licence; some of the more aspiring abstract names are missing from the Yorkshire list!*]

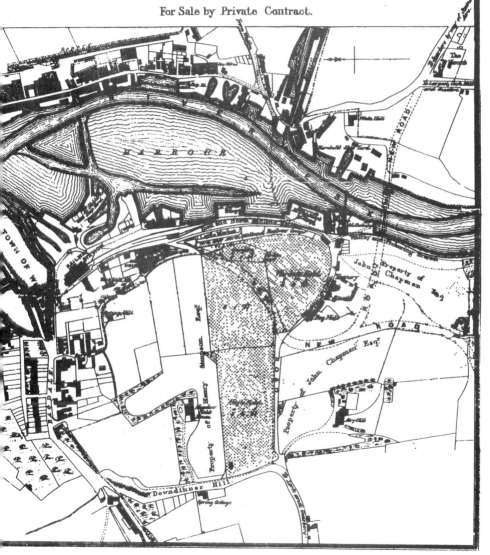

Whitby was the port which provided more ships than any other, and this map shows the extent of the ship-building that still prevailed in the town. (RB)

CHAPTER 5

Paul's *de facto* withdrawal from the Coalition meant that all the Russian soldiers stationed with the armies of the other Allies had to be repatriated. Thus there arrived in Cronstadt, as Commander of one of the many Cartels (ships transferring prisoners to exchange under a written agreement), one Lieutenant Norris R.N., who, despite an initially hostile reception, took the opportunity thus afforded for a little espionage, and on 19 October, 1800, sent back a description of the Russian Naval Fleet which must have inestimably cheered their Lordships in the Admiralty. On 19 October he described:

> *as truly as Crazy a Rotten Fleet as ever put to sea...The day prior to their being to sail, the Captains of Seven Line of Battle Ships made Reports, that the Ships were not fit to go out of the Mole, as they were then making six feet of water a day.*

However, more chillingly, he also described the extreme fear of the British merchants of being sent to Siberia.

By now the Tsar had declared Stephen Shairp *persona non grata*. His brother Alexander remained in Russia, and Stephen, a shrewd and gifted man, continued his Consular work from his London house at 73, Gower Street. Diplomatic relations had effectively ended. However, Stephen used his time to write long analyses of Russian trading methods to add to the detailed reports he was accustomed to sending to the Foreign Office. He made a determined effort to return to his post, urged by his ambassador, Lord Whitworth, who had withdrawn to Copenhagen. He set out in the lugger *Resolution*, which would be about 50 tons, not built for luxury, and he used a mixture of land and sea transport to reach St. Petersburg, where he was allowed to land. However, within days he was deported on the Tsar's orders. His claim for expenses, submitted to the Foreign Office on his return, details the difficulties inherent in international travel in a Europe beset by war and shifting alliances, and without a proper infrastructure of communications. One cannot but feel that the wine would be very necessary, given the poor state of water storage on board ship, and the extreme discomfort of the voyage.

Statement of the Expenses of Stephen Shairp on his voyage to Russia and back in the Lugger *Resolution* 1800; (PRO \ FO65 \ 47)

Chaise and Four from London to Deal, driver &c	£12.00.00
Wine, Provisions, &c at Elsineur	10.00.00
Chaise to Copenhagen, &c	6.00.00
Expenses at Cronstadt, Messengers to St Petersburg, Horses and Chaise, waiting &c 7 days about	20.00.00
Wine and Provisions for Voyage home	15.00.00
A Messenger dispatched from Rendsburg in Holstein to Lord Whitworth at Copenhagen	15.00.00
Landing at Yarmouth, pilot &c	4.00.00
Chaise from Yarmouth to London	11.00.00
Presents to the Master, Mate and Crew of the Lugger	30.00.00
A pilot engaged from Elsineur to Cronstadt & back	35.00.00
Pilots, horses &c in the River Eyder	10.16.00

NB: £40.16 of these two last sums have been claimed at the Navy Office but are not yet paid. **Total:** £168.16.00

The 'presents' to the crew of the lugger, which may well have been a naval transport, represented quite an outlay, and may have been an addition to naval wages. Alexander Shairp, meanwhile, acted as Vice-Consul. On 27 October (Old Style), the embargo was re-imposed, at both Cronstadt and Riga. This was the 'snare' in which were trapped the 22 ships loading Government stores at Riga, as well as the *George* and many others. At the same time Shairp reported that Paul was offering the Russian merchants frigates from the Russian Navy to carry their goods. In view of Lieut. Norris' report on the condition of the Russian Imperial Navy, that was a gift horse with very dubious teeth!

Ports involved in the Baltic and other northern European trades developed architectural styles which formed visual links between them. Here are crow-stepped gables in Whitby, though not as elegant or common as those which prevail in Fifeshire. (RB)

Another kind of gable found in Whitby. (RB)

Crowsteps in Dysart. (RB)

The fruits of success; these elegant 18th-century houses are in Whitby, and were occupied by some of the investors in shipping. (RB)

Many of these neat small houses in Cliff Street, Whitby, were occupied by the master mariners of the town. (RB)

CHAPTER 6

The sailors who were on board the newly embargoed vessels were then taken ashore for deportation, and it was at that point that Thomas Etty began to keep his Journal:

Thomas Etty's Book - December 15th. 1800

This was wrote in the Town of Fellin in Russia 211 Warses from Riga and 152 from Reval (Note. 1 Werse is equal to Three Quarters of an English Mi[le])

[Page 2]: *December 1 1800. The foregoing Journal is to testify, whom it may or doth concern that I, Thomas Etty and the rest of the Ship's Crew was under the same Command of Capt. T. Coverdale as when on board the Ship* George *by an Order from the Emperour of Russia.*

[Page 3]: *A Journal Containing a few Remarks that happened since the 1st of December 1800, on which day the Ship's Companies was ordered out of their Respective Ships (amongst which was the* George *of Whitby to whom I belong'd then laying at Bulroye Quay) in order to be marched to Riga. Monday 1st December 1800 about 11 o'clock in the forenoon was mustered and our Names called over by the Officers of the Regiment that was to conduct us to Riga, about 2 O'Clock in the Afternoon set out for Riga under a strong Guard of Soldiers about 5 the same Day arrived at Riga was mustered again ..d our Names called over by the*

[Page 4] [Page damaged]: *...n we was put into a dark prison nothing to sleep on but hard boards and no allowance whatever from the Russians, so that we was obliged to take what provisions we could get from our Ships in order to serve us till we got to our Journey's end as they would not find us with anything till then,) but let us return to our former Subject. Concerning the Dark Prison were we remained till Wednesday the 3rd 1800. There was prepared upwards of 50 Waggons each containing 1 Small Horse and some two, Those Waggons was to carry the luggage belonging to the Captains and Sailors, There was also 3 Carravans or Cover'd waggon each containgng four Horses. Those Caravans was*

[Page 5] [Page damaged]: *for the Captains to ride w... chused, a man was also appointed from every Ships company to go and lead the Waggons and to stay by them in order to take care of the luggage that belong'd to his Ship to see that the Russians did not commit any thefts as they are very light finger'd Gentry. Wednessday December 3 about 6 o'clock in the Afternoon Orders came for the Prisoners to march away that Night. According to order we got ready to March, and was mustered again, and was conducted by a strong guard of Russian Soldiers through Riga Town and preceeded on our Journey about 10 werses that Night when we came to a single house were we stayed all the Night to sleep but not much*

[Page 6] [Page damaged]: *...was to be got for the house was very small and very hot by reason of so many people being in it all together their was upwards of two hundred people taking Soldiers and Altogether for some got all the Straw that we had to Sleep upon and others got none at all and some lay one upon another so what one thing and what another their was very little rest all the Night through. Morning came at last waggons and horses was ordred to be shifted And to proceed on our Journey along with the same guard of Soldiers as before all the Waggons and Horses was shifted except the three Caravans and they was to continue so untill our Journey's End so thus ends the first stage.*

Shortly afterwards a *ukaase* or decree was issued to appoint a Board to liquidate all the 'concerns' between British and Russian Merchants. The exact sequence of events is very difficult to follow through diplomatic and other archives. There were two different calendars in existence. Russia still adhered to the 'Old Style' abandoned in Britain in 1752. This was eleven days out of alignment with the Gregorian Calendar, or 'New Style', used in England. Letters from Russia were dated sometimes in one and sometimes in another. In addition post was, at the very least, slow, and often interrupted by hostilities and their side-effects. Letter-writers did not always make clear which style of date they were using. Letters and orders frequently crossed. Even Thomas Etty was affected by this confusion as he endeavoured to sort out which day was Christmas Day at the end of 1800.

Thursday 25th December 1800 This being Christmas Day with us
[Page 20]: *But it is not regarded in the least by the people of this place as they thought no more of it than another Day. Thick foggy weather towards the Evening [Interpolation] Under command of our Captains as before.*

However, in due course, the alleged reasons for Paul's action became apparent, by means of letters from members of his Court. Paul's officials and courtiers continued a diplomatic correspondence with Britain through neutral channels. The details of the enormity of Paul's treatment of the seamen, and of the efforts made in Russia to alleviate their sufferings were also revealed . Although informed opinion became aware that the cause was the supposed personal affront over Malta, a further excuse was announced by *ukaase*.

The *ukaase* blamed the seizure some years earlier, in 1793 and 1795, of two ships belonging to Russian merchants, the *Alexander and Constantin*, and the *City of Amsterdam*. Both had been condemned as prizes, and the owners of both ships and cargo compensated at the usual rates. However, *ukaases* issued through the College of Commerce in St. Petersburg, at the time of the embargo, levied on the merchants of the St Petersburg Factory of the Russia Company a huge penalty, 104,000 Roubles, which they had to produce instantly, despite the fact that their trade had all been embargoed, and that Russian merchants were forbidden to trade with them. Each House had to collect up as much as it could raise in cash. The money collected was to be paid to one Christian Trompowski, a nobleman and shipowner. A further claim of about a quarter of a million Roubles was made by a merchant called Thomas Zuckerbecker, and that was to be settled by the sale of the ships seized in the embargo.

The name of *Zuckerbecker* was to be misinterpreted by the deported sailors when the alarming news filtered through to them:

Saturday December 27th 1800 Thick Cloudy weather, with a little snow towards Evening, &c. This Evening received Intelligence by private Letters that Six of the best Ships laying at Bullroye Quay, the Emperor of Russia has given them to a Sugar Maker *that lives at Petersburg for old Debts (amongst which was the* George *of Whitby) but this is not asserted for truth yet, as we expect to hear more about it in a Short time. (Under Command as before)*

The British record makes quite clear that both claimants had already been compensated legally for their losses, so that this charge was clearly 'trumped up', in the eyes of both the British Government and the Russia Company, as well as in the eyes of the press. It was a huge financial blow, to the British merchants on 'that side the water', and it must also have affected the Russian economy because of the cessation of a very lucrative trade.

A list survives of the moneys collected from the British counting houses in Russia:

List of British Merchants, and amounts paid by each to Russia during the embargo, 1800-01:

(PRO / FO65 / 48)

Merchant	*Sum Collected*
Paris Warre Harvey	*Ro 35,000.00.00*
Thomson Boncer	*23,535.79*
Thornton Cayley	*15,000.00*
Shairp's	*7,000.00*
Porter Brown Wilson	*5,000.00*
Thornton Bayley	*5,200.00*
Timothy Raihes [sic]	*1,000.00*
Anderson and Moberley	*3,000.00*
W.C.J. Venning	*3,000.00*
William Glen	*2,000.00*
Carr Goddard	*15,000.00*
	104,235.79
	(should be): 114,535.79
	(Ro=Roubles)

Yet Russia was so vast and had such huge resources that, despite the chaotic ineptitude of her government and the instability of the Tsar, she could afford to impose such penalties on herself as well as those she deemed to have offended her, and she was for that reason a most formidable enemy.

A top-sail schooner with an ordinary schooner moored alongside her. Both have two masts, but only the left hand one has any square sails. Further over is a barque, with three masts, two square-rigged and one, the mizzen, fore-and-aft rigged. (FMS)

The Earl of Mulgrave (left), and members of his family; the Earl, of Mulgrave Castle, near Whitby, had a distinguished military career, and was M.P. for Scarborough before he succeeded his elder brother. He later became Foreign Secretary, in 1805. He had extensive interests in shipping, and during his term of office a second Baltic confrontation, this time with Tsar Alexander I, took place. (TE)

LUGGER

When Stephen Shairp made his long voyage to St Petersburg in the autumn of 1800, it was in a lugger such as this. It could sail close to the wind, but could be unstable in a gale with her large sails set. (WLP)

CHAPTER 7

Much of the correspondence about these matters came through letters to the Russia Company, via courageous messengers who crossed throughout the winter in both directions. Appeals to the British Government for recompense of expenses are to be found in the public records. They were, to Government's credit, granted. The extorted money was found, and the Factory continued its now precarious existence in an enemy country of considerable volatility. 'This side the water' Stephen Shairp carried on producing his reports, filtering details from networks of correspondence which amount to espionage. There is a curiously exciting immediacy about finding, in a letter book of 1801, a carefully decoded letter in a number-cipher, groups of four numbers in neat columns. Departing diplomats were instructed to burn their code books, and, in due course, when diplomatic links were restored letters were sent to the new embassy in plain language, full of diplomatic phrases, but accompanied by other secret letters, in new replacement codes, couched in much more forceful terms.

Meanwhile, by means of an Order in Council issued at the Court of St. James, on 14 January, 1801, an embargo was placed on the shipping of Russia and her new allies in the so-called Northern Confederacy, Denmark and Sweden, found in British waters. Military plans were laid for some kind of retaliation. The virtual non-existence of Russia's merchant fleet meant that only one Russian ship was seized, the *Angolo*, and the brunt fell on Sweden and Denmark, her allies in the Northern Confederacy. Four Danish ships were captured by the frigate HMS *Amazon* and sent into Hull, and HM Sloop-of-War *Squirrel* sent two Swedish ships, one bound for the Mediterranean with naval stores, into Hull, and three into Great Yarmouth. The inhabitants of both ports, knowing that their own ships had been captured by the Russian allies of Sweden and Denmark, must have viewed these crews a little askance, though probably no more than they would have done French prisoners, their more frequent guests. The Government reacted with great anger to the deportation of the crews, particularly as the enormity of their probable plight in the Russian winter became clearer after the winter journey back to England of Alexander Shairp, with details of the seamen's condition. What we might now recognise as the 'Falklands Factor' came into existence, as a class of men, merchant seamen, hitherto taken much for granted save as a source of skilled labour for the Navy, often exploited by their owners and masters, and frequently captured by French warships and privateers, suddenly became the victims of a *cause célèbre*. There is, however, a thread of humanity which runs through all the papers from all sources at this period, as national and local officials, press, merchants and ordinary people combined to ease the lot of those who had been captured, and those who were bereft of both information and livelihood at home.

When the crew-members were taken from their ships it was not to be imprisoned locally as prisoners of war: it was to be 'deported' to the interior of Russia. In all, between the two principal ports of St. Petersburg and Riga, some 2,000 seamen from some 200 ships were sent off to 102 different destinations in Russia, to be followed after a few weeks by the 400 mates and boys who had been left behind. There was, of course, no Geneva Convention at this time, but there were accepted practices. Generally officers were given parole, and allowed to live within the community, unless, of course, as some did, they refused to give their word not to escape. Other ranks involved in an embargo would be kept, uncomfortably, in prisons or naval barracks until they could be exchanged. In the earlier embargo in Russia, however, they had been put into barracks without food, but only a supply of water and wood, for twenty-four hours.

Normally if they were captured in sea battles or skirmishes, they might indeed be marched to a suitable prison, but the usual enemy was France, and France was neither bitterly cold nor far from home. Although by the later stages of the War many prisoners were exchanged by cartel within a month of capture, many merchant seamen spent long periods of the Napoleonic Wars in prison camps and fortresses, and many were to die there, mainly in France, as at Verdun, Arras, Auxerre, Valenciennes, Givet and Cambrai, but some in America, when that country joined with France later in the War. The horror that resulted from the Russian incident was caused by the alien nature of much of that great empire, and by the known intensity of winter cold, and the vast distances to be walked. Added to that was the righteous rage that this imprisonment should be imposed by a supposed ally on such flimsy excuses. Even the alphabet was alien in Russia. Thomas Etty might comment that the local language was what he identified as German, but such signs as the prisoners did see would have been in the Cyrillic alphabet, so that it became exceedingly difficult to identify from the few letters home that did filter through exactly where they were imprisoned. This makes the historian's task equally difficult!

Normally the capturing power gave subsistence to its prisoners, but as the initial part of Thomas' Journal made clear:

no allowance whatever from the Russians, so that we was obliged to take what provisions we could get from our Ships in order to serve us till we got to our Journey's end as they would not find us with anything till then,

this was not to be the Russian practice. The prisoners' own government, acting through well-paid agents who lived and worked openly and officially in the relevant country, provided cash for extras at specific rates, carefully tailored to rank, and therefore to expectation. A letter from the Admiralty Transport Office to Alexander Shairp, dated 25 February, 1801, offers the view, after allowing his expenses for the work he had done, *that the Allowance made by the Russian Government to the Persons in question is sufficient for their subsistence; and, as it is not probable that they will immediately want any further Supply of Clothing, the only Expense that is now to be incurred on behalf of this Country appears to be the daily Allowance of three Pence to each Master and Mate, and three-halfpence to each Seaman...*

Letters home from masters confirm the lack of subsistence from the Russians, and show their dependence on the kindness of the Russia Company's merchants.

When an *Arrête*, a decree of annulment, from the French Government, of November, 1799, ended the supply of extra food and tobacco to French prisoners in England, there was much disquiet within the British Government, because the reaction of the French prisoners was to sell their meagre clothing in order to purchase tobacco, so that many of them were in a very distressed state. The Government felt aggrieved at this pressure put on Britain to provide extra support for enemy prisoners. However, the treatment of prisoners tended to be unsystematic, changing as it did from one treaty to another. Paul I, however, did not even play according to the 'norms' of 1800.

Ordinarily the ships caught in the final embargo would have been safely away from the Gulf of Riga well before the date on which the crews were taken off, but there had been the earlier embargo, with its enforced unloading of cargo, and then the reloading after it was called off. Additionally the British Government had refused permission for ships to sail for the Baltic, so that the last convoy arrived very late and was still loading. Despite the fact that the men themselves were clothed for an active shipboard life, rather than a long slow march through a bitter Russian winter, Paul I sent them off in divisions to march into the interior. He was himself a man obsessed with the concept of marching, and was known to drill his household troops to the point of exhaustion.

Thomas Etty described his division, including guards, as about 200 men and boys. Of the 102 destinations stipulated, some were as much as 1,300 *vjersts*, or 1,000 miles, distant. The men were divided into groups of ten men to one Captain, the Mates being left behind to guard the ships. Many of the ships which had been caught in the previous embargo would therefore be short of supplies. Indeed there is evidence that merchants had to lend money to the Captains to purchase supplies for the march. Although the trip could take up to two months, the pressure of the war had reduced that sharply, and with it the need for ships to carry large quantities of supplies. Worse than that, many of the men would have no walking shoes. Seamen did not march, as Thomas light-heartedly made clear:

3 O'Clock in the Affternoon was march at the Entrance of the Town were we was placed in two ranks like as many Soldiers, in this position we was order'd to march into the Town, but you may easily guess how long we should keep in two ranks, for we had not march'd five minutes before all was confusion, as this manner of walking rank and file was quiet contrary to what we had been used to, so it was a very tedious piece of work for the Soldiers to place us in two ranks in order to count us, this was the hardest Jobb they had.

and Captain Ward of the *Fishburn* described his group as 'barefoot'. Many of the 'seamen' were boys, since as much as a quarter of each ship's crew might consist effectively of children, still growing, and much more vulnerable to cold and hunger than adults, because of their tendency to lose body heat more quickly. There may even have been some girls among the travellers, and some women, as Masters, particularly of the smaller vessels, often lived and raised their families on board ship, going ashore only for the winter lay-up. One must hope that the pressures of war and the dangers of the summer had reduced the number of 'passengers'. Thomas recounted in his Journal that the crews were accompanied by carts pulled by small horses, with all their possessions loaded upon them, and that there was great need to guard these carts diligently to prevent the Russian soldiers from pilfering goods, particularly food.

Thursday 4 Dec...was station'd to every Waggon as it was found ... too tedious for one man to attend 3 or 4 Waggons as the Russians was continually commiting some small Theft or other, particularly our provisions was their chief Object, so we proceeded on our Journey till the Evening when we came to a single house and slept upon Straw shifted our baggage waggons and horses every stage as before

When one considers the quality of ship-board food at that time and the nature of ship's bread, particularly when infested with weevils and 'bargemen', then the Russian soldiers must have been in equally hard straits. In Thomas' division caravans, or covered wagons, pulled by better horses, were provided for the Captains, so that they might ride. This is confirmed in a letter from a Captain from Hull in another division, who wrote re-assuringly to his family about their comfort, although many of the 're-assuring ' letters were, as Captain William Cramp wrote, composed under censorship. However, the merchants left in Russia were not so sanguine of the seamen's chances of survival. Letters were sent to the British Government asking how much the men were to be paid in extra allowances, and stating the normal Russian subsistence pay. In Cronstadt, Alexander Shairp, out of his own pocket, and imitated by other merchants in Riga, though no details from that port have survived, paid for each man to be provided with a sheepskin coat, hat, and gloves, together with a pair of boots and two pairs of socks. It was a considerable achievement, given the chaotic state of commerce in Russia. Nevertheless, Alexander wrote despairingly of seeing so many off to what he feared would be death by the roadside.

It is to the great credit of the British Government that, when his appeal came through, he was immediately recompensed and allowed money with which to subsidise the seamen in their imprisonment, although the letter, already quoted, is worded with bureaucratic caution. He also gave to each Master 200 roubles, against his receipt, for payment to his crew, at a rate of about ten men to each Master. This money had been provided by one of the Counting Houses of the Russia Company, despite the demands which had already been made of them for money to recompense Trompowski and Zuckerbecker. The Merchants did their best to enable the survival of the men during this ordeal. That became clear from other letters published in the *Hull Advertiser* and other newspapers of the day. We know, of course, that men did die, though there are none named. Letters in the Foreign Office archives record:

They appeared in tolerable spirits, and made no complaints: but I am sorry to say that several have died on their march, and were buried at different places on the road.

Men would die of cold, of disease, of exhaustion and possibly of fear. Not all Masters would be fair or humane men, or even competent to cope with such an incident as this. Captain Thomas Coverdale allocated money carefully, as is shown by Thomas Etty's own accounts,

[Page 78]		*Copeaks*	
Monday	*Dec. 15th. 1800*	*Received*	*72*
Tuesday	*Dec. 16th. 1800*		*12*
Wednesday	*Dec. 17th. 1800*	*for 8 Days*	*100*
Tuesday	*Dec. 23rd. 1800*	*for 6 Days*	*105*
Monday	*Dec. 29th. 1800*		*135*
Monday	*Jan. 5th. 1801*		*106*
Tuesday	*Jan. 13th. 1801*		*50*
Wednesday	*Jan. 14th. 1801*		*85*
Tuesday	*Jan. 20th. 1801*		*35*
Wednesday	*Jan. 21st. 1801*		*100*
Thursday	*Jan. 22nd. 1801*		
Received from Mr. Coverdale			*145*
this was the overplus Money sent from the Merchants			
Wednesday	*Jan. 28th. 1801*		*35*
Thursday	*Jan. 29th. 1801*		*135*
Wednesday	*Feby. 4th. 1801*	*Rec.*	*35*
Friday	*Feb. 6th. 1801*	*Rece. 131,*	*60+70*
Friday	*Feb. 13th. 1801*	*Rece.*	*70*
Wednesday	*Feb. 18th. 1801*		*50*
Thursday	*Feb. 19th. 1801*		*50*
Saturday	*Feb. 21st. 1801*		*170*
[Page 79]		*Copeaks*	
Saturday	*Feb. 28th. 1801*		*70*
Friday	*March 6th. 1801*		*70*
Wednesday	*March 11th. 1801*		*100*
Saturday	*March 14th*	*140,*	*70+70*
Saturday	*March 21st.*	*120,*	*50+70*
Saturday	*March 28th.*		*70*
Tuesday	*March 31st.*		*150*

Saturday	April 4th.		241
Sunday	April 5th.		30
Monday	13th.		70
Friday	17th.	Lent	50
Monday	20th.		70
Friday	April 24th.	Lent	50
Monday	April 27th.	Lent	100
	Money		

[Page 80] *from 23rd of September 1800 to August 7th 1801*

M[onths]	D[ays]
10	14
4	18
5	28

and other Masters wrote home of their care for their crews, but some would fail, or their men and boys would not trust them, and those crewmen who were weak, or poorly supported, would succumb. At the other end of the scale were the old men, of whom there would be quite a few, prematurely aged by the rigorous life, unable to afford to retire because of financial misfortune (or incompetence), and recruited to fill gaps left by the press-gang. They were supposed to be able to ride with the sick in the covered wagons. To force seamen, short of walking experience, brought up on an island with a temperate climate – however well they might tolerate the cold winds which blew at sea – to march up to 1,000 miles into the interior of Russia during the winter was to invite disaster. The worst of the despair would have come when word filtered through, as it did to Thomas' division in Fellin, that the ships had been sold.

It would be one thing for seamen to be aware, as indeed they would be, that, if their ships were taken as prizes by the French, then the crews would possibly be exchanged under Cartel; it was quite another to be trapped in the vast Russian interior where the sea was so far distant, the language incomprehensible, and the weather bitter beyond anything they had ever imagined. Only those who had survived overwintering in the Arctic ice with the whaling fleet would be aware that such cold could exist. Even Thomas, ex-whale-fisher, said,

I never felt it so cold in all my life.

The port with the second highest list of missing men was Hull, where the Mayor managed to raise over £1,300 for relief, from a population of 22,000. Here is an early view of the castle at Hull.

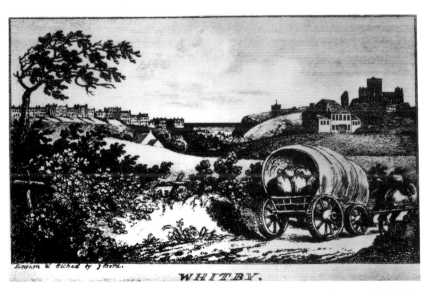

WHITBY.

In Thomas' Journal he refers to caravans for the Captains. They were covered wagons, of which this is a North Riding version. (TE)

CHAPTER 8

By the time Thomas dated the first page of the small, roughly stitched book wrapped in a sacking cover, some of his compatriots has already been on the road for some time. The first deportations from Cronstadt seem to have begun on 15 November as soon as the embargo was in place. Indeed there is evidence that Alexander Shairp had already made contingency plans. The first contingent of British seamen left Riga for Wenden on the 22nd.

On 28 November Captain Thornton of the *Nymph*, of Dundee, wrote from Wolmar, describing a five-day march and giving news of the safety of himself and four other Masters, two from Dysart and two from Dundee, with their crews. He described the Russian Government's allowance as a 'scanty pittance', and praised the Riga merchants for their help. The ill behaviour of some crewmen may have led indirectly to the existence of Thomas' little journal, since Thomas stated that it was kept on an order from the Emperor to show that he and the crew were 'under command'. Captain Thornton praised his Russian guards, and indicated that they were on the whole well treated, and had some freedom of movement about the town.

The immediate response to the first news of the prisoners' conditions was an order from Henry Dundas, the Secretary for War, to the agents working for the relief of prisoners of war in France. The agents were ordered to cease immediately the supply of provisions for Russian prisoners. One must wonder what distress that caused to men so far from home, and quite powerless to affect the Tsar's whims in regard to British seamen.

Thomas Etty's group was mustered at 11 o'clock on 1 December, ordered from the ships, and marched towards Riga under *'a strong guard of soldiers'*. By the 8th, after several uncomfortable nights, and the constant anxiety about theft from their scanty provisions,

> *arrived at a small Town called Wolmer This being the first Town that we saw since our first Leaving Riga in this Town was several English Sailors that was billited out at different houses according to the Circumstances of the people that kept it. These Sailors belonged to the second Division that was sent up in the Country. This was the only place that we came to were we could buy any provisions, there was none to be bought on the road neither for love nor Money if we had been perishing with hunger, here we renewed our stock of provisions, that it might*

[Page 9] [Page damaged] *not fail before we got to our Journey's end. This Night shifted our baggage Waggons and Horses in order to go away very early in the Morning. Tuesday 9th December About four O'Clock in the Morning was called up to get ready for Marching about 5 O'clock set forward on our Journey under the same guard of Soldiers as before.*

The sailors they met were no doubt the Scottish men mentioned by Captain Thornton, including those who had nearly ended up in prison for riotous behaviour. There at least they were able to improve their foodstuffs.

Meanwhile, Captain Bunney of Hull, Master of the *Mary Frances*, wrote to his wife from Novgorod, en route to Moscow, on 3 December, 1800:

I arrived here this day, and travel from hence in the morning on the road to Moscow. We have found every civility from our Officer and the inhabitants on the road, and was never in better health in my life; we have not had the least fatigue, as we walk or ride as we please. My men and boys are with me and are well and in good spirits; Captains Wood and Brown of Hull are in our division and captains Bowser and Atkinson, also of Hull, join us every third night on the march. We have tea and coffee twice a day, and one good stew of meat or poultry, which is in great plenty and very reasonable. The Merchants in Petersburg, we shall never be able to repay for their kindness, for they strove who should do the most to serve us; when we set off they furnished us with money and victuals in abundance, and every other accommodation to make us comfortable. Shall write to you again on my arrival in Moscow, (which I expect will be about the 1st of January), where I have a number of friends, and my ship's company shall have every assistance and comfort that I can procure them.

This letter to Captain Bunney's wife was published in the *Hull Advertiser* of 17 January, 1801, to allay the town's fears about the fate of the seamen. One wonders what the 'boys', cold, tired and hungry, made of one meal a day, and two cups of tea or coffee! Was this letter censored, edited by the newspaper to serve a point, or composed by Captain Bunney to soothe his wife. At least it was news, though, to the seamen's wives struggling to make ends meet without their husbands' pay, the one meat or poultry stew must have seemed ironic.

On the 8th of the same month, Alexander Shairp, having made all his enquiries, wrote to the Government to say that some 200 ships had been captured. An editorial in the *Hull Packet*, on which Thomas' brother William Etty was an apprentice, appeared on 9 December, and put the disaster into context for the town of Hull:

The inhabitants of London (the nobles and the gentry) are men of landed, rather than commercial property. In Hull all are commercial: the merchant connected with the banker, and the shop-keeper with both. London and Newcastle obtain a credit with other towns and other nations: Hull is in advance with Russia and gives a credit to Russia. In Liverpool the Baltic insurances are very few; in Hull they amount to hundreds of thousands of pounds... The loss of this town from a Russian war would be greater than the loss of any other city or town in the island.

However, it is doubtful whether the owners at Whitby, from which almost twice as many ships as from Hull were captured, would have agreed with him, The loss in gross terms might have been the largest, but, in proportion to the population, some much smaller ports, such as those in Scotland, may have been desperately badly affected.

This view of the old graving dock at Whitby would have been familiar to Thomas, as would the feeling of anticipation as his ship sailed down the Esk to the sea. (FMS)

CHAPTER 9

The actual conditions under which the men walked must have varied according to the distance and time taken, and the kind of weather that the divisions met. Thomas Etty found the roads poor, and was extremely scornful of the construction methods used. Given the poor state of 18th-century roads in England, the Russian ones must therefore have been very much worse.

Wednesday 10th December. Got our waggons and horses shifted very early in the Morning. From this time the roads was very bad and very heavey, occasion'd by a sudden Thaw as the high road for several Werses is Nothing but light Sand, (their Method of Repairing the high Road is thus, were they find a place that wants levelling they go and cut down the Fir Trees
[Page 10] *that grow by the road side as this part of the Country abounds with them, lops of all the branches and then lays them athwart the road, upon these they lay the small branches, and upon the Branches, they lay a great Quantity of loose yellow sand according as they think proper, so that in rainy weather the Waggons sink up to the very Axletree in Dirt.*

John Agar, Mate and later Master of the *Ploughman*, wrote to his wife in Whitby on 10 January, having arrived at Tver on 20 December, after walking 442 miles from St Petersburg. The letter was apparently calculated to alleviate anxiety and indicates that food was adequate and affordable. It contained information about as many of his colleagues among the other Masters as possible,

Captains Dickinson and Appleton are of our division, but are quartered (the former) 40 and the latter 60 miles from this place, but our captains frequently have letters from them; they are very well.
John Oxley, with Captain Sharp of Hull, are well; Captains Dale and Ellerby were well on the 15th ult. We parted with them about five days' march from here; they are gone 200 miles further than this; Captain Pearson of Hull, and Captain ... of Whitby are well and set off this morning; they are going almost 400 miles farther. The carpenter of the Harpooner has been ill of a fever, but is recovering fast; we attend him every day, and get him a little tea, which is the only thing we are allowed to take into the hospital. Captains Waite and Hutchinson of Whitby passed through this place, all well.

By the time John Agar arrived at Tver, Thomas Etty and his division had arrived at Fellin, on December 15th, but not without some trouble other than the state of the roads.

37

Thomas Etty spent the last fifty years of his life in Hull, living in Church Lane, where he pursued his trade as a wholesale confectioner and ginger-bread maker. During the bombing in 1941 much of the Old Town was destroyed, including Church Lane. This is all that remains, the Staithe to the Old Harbour. The far warehouse would have been there in Thomas' time. (RB)

Trinity House, Hull, established as a guild in 1369, and chartered as an independent corporation in 1541, when Henry VIII visited Hull with Queen Catherine Howard. It was and is responsible for charitable purposes and maritime duties in Hull. This is its fine 18th-century facade, relatively new in Thomas' day. (RB)

Thursday 11th. December 1800

Arose very early in the Morning got our waggons and horses shifted proceeded on our Journey with the same guard of Soldiers as before. This Day a Serjant belonging to the company of Soldiers that conducted us all the way, struck at several of the Sailors and begun to treat us worse than usual, one man in particular he struck several times and used him very ill, but however the man said nothing as

[Page 11] it was no use to talk to them as they could not speak a word of English, but walked on before the baggage Waggons and soon came up with the Caravans were the Captains rode, and told them of the ill treatment that he had received from the Serjeant without cause, the Captains soon inform'd Mr. Moore a Gentleman that went with us as an Interpreter, that is to Resolve any Questions that may be required on both Sides, as he could speak several Languages. Our Interpreter soon inform'd the Captain of the Russian Soldiers of the above cause, who said that he would not suffer any of his Inferiour Officers to Molest the English Men upon no Account, unless without cause, therefore he determined to call a court Martial and have him flogged at the first house we came to. Accordingly marched on a few Werses

[Page 12] farther, we came to a large house were the Caravans stop'd and all the baggage waggons, Soldiers and Sailors likewise. Accordingly a Court Martial was call'd the Serjeant was brought in before the Captain to speak for himself. the sailor was also called to appear against him, the man stripped himself and shewed the Marks & bruises upon his back, this condemned him without any more ceremony so that he could say nothing for himself, But however he was pardoned this time, and bound over for his good behaviour never to Molest the English Men any more.

The terrain began to oppress Thomas as they walked through the seemingly endless pine forests of the great European plain, sleeping little since the few habitations were far too small to accommodate so many in comfort. The roads improved as the weather worsened simply because the unstable mixture of timber and sand froze hard, and was easier to walk on. The sandy soil of the northern plain, with its vast silent forests would have been very eerie to men from the varied terrain of Britain. To the present author as a 12-year-old child, going to live in northern Germany in 1946 was a great surprise, and she did not have to trudge endlessly through it in the middle of winter without metalled roads.

Thomas' arrival in Fellin provided an outlet for his dry sense of humour, as the guarding soldiers tried to improve their appearance by marching them into the town in an orderly manner.

3 O'Clock in the Affternoon was march at the Entrance of the Town were we was placed in two ranks like as many Soldiers, in this position we was order'd to march into the Town, but you may easily guess how long we should keep in two ranks, for we had not march'd five minutes before all was confusion, as this

*manner of walking rank and file was quiet contrary to what we had been used
to, so it was a very tedious piece of work for the Soldiers to place us in two ranks
in order to count us, this was the hardest Jobb they had.*

There the paper work and the billeting began; there was no barracks, no camp
for them. One wonders what the ordinary people on whom they were billeted
thought at having this miscellaneous division of foreign seamen invade their
houses, ill-found in cash, speaking none of their languages.

*Saturday 13th December 1800 Changed our waggons and horses early in the
Morning got ready for Marching it was told amongst us that this was to be the
last Stage, you may easily conceive that we was well pleased to hear this News
as we was rather fatigued with travelling so far, never sleeping on a bed from
our first being taken out of the*
[Page 14] *Ships at Bullroye Quay. About half past Three arrived at the
Custom house to receive our Instruction. Here a Ships Name was called over
as set down on the list and the Ships Company*
[Page 15] *that belonged to that Ship was sent in a Room before 4 Officers
were they wrote down their Names their Ages their Complexion and the colour
of their Hair, this being done another ships Crew was called on and past through
the same examination till all was done, After this 2 Ships was called at once,
their Number of Men set down, and what place they were to go to, and how many
to a house &c. This being done we went along with an Officer, were he
distributed us about like hand bills some 2 to one house some 4, some 6, and
some 8 Men to an house according to the circumstances of the people.*

Thomas and another young man, possibly a shipmate, found themselves
billeted with a cabinet-maker, and set about 'housekeeping'. 'Housekeeping'
on 12½ copeks a day was a struggle, for a lad who might never have had to
contend with the problem in his life.

*Here our Allowance was only small it was 12 and half Copeaks per day or
1 Ruble for 8 Days which is 100 Copeaks. This is equal to half a crown for Eight
Days, Beef was 5 Copeaks per pound, bread and every other Article was very
dear, so that with*
[Page 16]
*our bare allowance we could scarce make two Meals a Day. The name of this
Town is Fellen otherwise Felen it is 211 Werses from Riga, and 152 from Reval.
(One of these Werses is equal to Three-quarters of an English Mile) it is seated
in a pleasant part of the Country, it stands upon a hill ... there is only one Church
in it, which has got a high small Spire and may be seen at a considerable
Distance most part of the houses are built of Fir wood. The Inhabitants in
General speak Dutch and* [interpolation] *are very Civil to Englishmen as long
as they behave themselves in a decent manner Saturday Night me and another
young man was billited at a Cabinet maker's house*

Sunday 14th December 1800 This Day past away without anything worth relating except it was a very hard frost, and we had very little to eat.

Monday 15th December begun house keeping at the rate of half a Crown per week. This Day received from Thos. Coverdale 12 Capeaks for 1 Days pay. This days payment was stopped [appears to have been faintly crossed out]

Tuesday 16th December This is what I call an Introduction to housekeeping, to learn to be frugal, This day received 12 Capeaks from my Captain for 1 Day's pay [there follow a few lines of apparent doodle such as one might put at the end of a page to fill it, and over this is written] *hard frosty Weather This Day's pay was also stoped.*

Received orders to Obey our Captains the same as when on board our ships
[Page 18]

Wednesday 17th December still continuing to freeze very hard I never felt it so cold in all my life. This day the Soldiers that conducted us from Riga is set out again to march all the way back to Riga again.

Received 1 Ruble or 100 Copeaks for to serve me Eight Days.

Thursday 18th December 1800. Thick cloudy weather still

It would seem that Thomas was reaping the reward of the ill-behaviour of some of the seamen at Wolmar, and possibly of some high spirits or rebellion of his own. Twice his pay was stopped. There is nothing to indicate whether that was a decision of Captain Coverdale or of the Russian authorities. They were back under ship's discipline, and control of the purse-strings was a powerful weapon. In wartime his wages as a seaman might well have been as high as £5 per month, some 3s 4d per day. The Russians expected him to survive on one rouble, 100 copeks, or 2s 6d per eight days, less than 4d per day, plus, when it percolated through the system, the 1½d allowed by the British Government. Even his peacetime wages would have been about 1s 8d per day, some four or five times as much as he now received. Captain Thornton at Wolmar was on roughly the same amount, but when Captain William Stephenson, of the Hull vessel *Flaxton*, wrote to his Owners, from St Petersburg in the following April, on his return from Staraya Russia, he reported that they had lived on five copeks, three halfpence, per day, basically the British allowance for 'extras'.

News filtered through to the prisoners, together with small amounts of extra cash, and Thomas listed each item painstakingly. The arrival of the mates and boys was a blow;

Saturday January 3rd 1801 This Morning arrived at this Town The Mates, likewise several Men and Boys that was left on board by order to take care of the Ships at Bullroye after the People was taken out.

He was puzzled by the calendar variations, but on the whole complained little about conditions apart from hunger and the weather. He certainly does not appear to have found the cruelty experienced by Captain Ward in Dorpat:

We are at this present time barefoot, and the cold is so intense that we cannot stir out of doors....the people (the crew) [are billeted] *on that of an old widow lady, who is totally divested of humanity.*

Captain Ward and the *Fishburn's* crew had no beatings, however, on their march, and tramped only a short distance. In a letter to the *Naval Chronicle* of early 1801, Stephen Shairp reported that some men had had to march up to 2,000 miles to prison. Allowing for propagandist exaggeration, many still marched for probably at least half of this distance, through varied weather. The Climatic Research Institute at the University of East Anglia has records of temperatures for parts of the Russian Empire in that year, and the temperature was for much of the time below average, while at others it was comparatively mild. It is impossible to generalise over such a vast geographical area.

Christmas, both the ignored 'English' one and the Russian one, came and went.

This Day was kept by the People of this Town, the same as the New Christmas Day in England.

March began, and by then Thomas' Journal had become very terse. Only his receipts and occasional cash were recorded. Very often he wrote only the date, to comply with the rules.

Sunday March 1st 1801 to Thursday 5th [date only]
Friday 6th. Saturday 7th Received from Mr Coverdale 70 Capeaks
Sunday 8th 1801 Monday 9th Began to build a Ship [interpolation]
Tuesday 10th Wednesday 11th. Received one Ruble
Thursday 12th Friday 13th March
Saturday 14th Received 70 Capeaks Emperors Money and 70 Capeaks Merchants Money

That Fellin, well inland, may have been a river port is shown by the presence of the Custom House, and by the tiny interpolation in the Journal on 9 March, when, more than three months into their captivity, Thomas wrote, very small, *'Began to build a ship'.*

What happened? One must assume they meant a full-size one, or there would have been no point in the apparent secrecy; sailors made model ships to pass their leisure time as a matter of course. Did the inhabitants, tired of the burden of supporting the seamen, or sickened by life under Paul, connive at an attempt to escape? Thomas was billeted with a cabinet-maker who would have had tools for working wood. The crews had their own possessions from the ship, presumably including implements, and there would have been shipwrights and carpenters amongst them. Every ship carried one or two, as well as sail-makers. There is, of course, a possibility that they were set to work by their captors to build ships, to help the Russian economy by providing for a merchant fleet. French prisoners in Whitby built a sail-factory a few years later.

Above: The two schooners tied up here are the Lively *and the* Mulgrave, *the latter built in 1786 and owned by Lord Mulgrave. The picture is interesting because of the extensive patching on the sails. Sails were patched until at times there was little left of the original cloth. Mulgrave was finally wrecked in 1888, 102 years old, so Thomas Etty and the other seamen would all have known her. (FMS)*

Left: Whitby Seamen's Hospital, the almhouses now hidden behind an elegant, early 19th-century facade by Gilbert Scott. (RB)

CHAPTER 10

On 'this side the water' activity on all fronts was prodigious. Letters continued to arrive in Whitehall and the City of London through neutral sources. The despairing Russia Company Merchants suggested using Prussian ports as outlets for their goods. £1,000 was paid to Alexander Shairp in February, through the free and neutral city of Hamburg, for the relief of the seamen. In the same month Alexander managed to visit England for consultations.

On 17 December the Russia Company Merchants had decided to set up a fund for the relief of the seamen and their dependants. That a similar fund existed in Whitby is revealed by a long and increasingly acrimonious correspondence [*NYCRO\ZWvi 11\10\1-9*] about whether Whitby owners should contribute to the main appeal as well as aiding their own. By 20 February they had sent £100 to add to the Lord Mayor's Fund which by then stood at nearly £7,000. In addition, they were supporting through the Poor Law and the Seamen's Fund the dependants of the Whitby seamen. On 24 January the *Hull Advertiser* reported that a performance at the Theatre Royal, Hull, of *Jane Shore* had raised over £26 to add to the £1,200 already raised by the Mayor of Hull.

In February, the Government decided to go to war. It would have been impossible to attack Russia by sea because the Baltic was likely to be frozen, but Russia's somewhat reluctant ally, Denmark, was accessible. Emissaries were sent to Denmark to deliver an ultimatum that she should abandon the Northern Confederacy, and on 4 March Sir Hyde Parker, Admiral of the Blue, stationed off Yarmouth, a port already involved in the crisis, with seven of its own ships captured, and sheltering embargoed Swedish vessels, received orders to sail for Copenhagen with Nelson as his Vice-Admiral. A copy of the orders to Admiral Sir Hyde Parker has survived among the Canning Papers in Leeds, sent, probably quite unofficially, to the out-of-office Foreign Affairs specialist George Canning. Cabinet leaks seem to be a long-standing phenomenon!

Copy of Instructions sent to Admiral Sir Hyde Parker, Commander-in-Chief, Fleet, 4 March, 1801.

Canning Papers, Leeds District Archives, West Yorkshire Archives. March 4th., 1801.

Whereas information has been received that a great number of Vessels belonging to His Majesty's(1) subjects have been and are detained in the Ports of Russia, and that their Crews have been and are now detained in the Ports, and that their Crews have been and are now detained as Prisoners of War in different parts of that Empire; and that during the continuance of these proceedings a confederacy (sic) of a hostile nature against the just rights and interests of His Majesty and his Dominions, has been entered into with the Court of St. Petersburg by the Courts of Denmark and Sweden respectively(2).

And whereas the Right Honourable Henry Dundas(3), One of His Majesty's Principal Secretaries of State, hath by his letter of the 23rd. of last month, signified to us His Majesty's pleasure that a Fleet should forthwith be sent off of Copenhagen, and that the Officer Commanding it on his arrival there should make such a disposition of the Ships under his Command as in his Judgement may appear most likely to ensure the success of the attempt it will be his duty to make (should all proposals for conciliation fail) to destroy the Arsenal of Copenhagen with the whole of the Shipping in that Port; and whereas we have thought fit to appoint you to the command of the Fleet prepared for this important service, You are in pursuance of His Majesty's pleasure signified as abovementioned hereby required and directed to proceed, without a moment's delay, with the Ships and Vessels mentioned on the other side hereof (or such of them as may be with you, leaving Orders for the remainder to follow) off of Copenhagen accordingly. On your arrival within the Categat, you are to send, with the proper and customary precautions, the letter (which accompanies this) from Lord Hawkesbury(4), One of His Majesty's Principal Secretaries of State, to Mr. Drummond, His Majesty's Minister Plenipotentiary at the Court of Denmark, informing him at the same time of your arrival with the force under your command, and of any other circumstances you may think it material for him to know; the principal subject of the above letter (as will be perceived by the copy thereof) being to direct Mr. Drummond to require an explicit and final answer from the Government of Denmark in the course of Forty-eight hours respecting any negotiations that may be then pending, and in case they should refuse within that time to acquiesce in such arrangement as he is authorised to propose and admit on the part of this Country, then to leave Copenhagen with all persons attached to his mission; you are to arrange with Mr. Drummond the most expeditious mode of your being apprized of the final decision of the Court of Denmark on this subject, and in the event of a convention not being signed and no assurance being received that it would be ratified immediately, according to the Instructions which have been given to Mr. Drummond and Mr. Vansittart(5) for that purpose or in case Mr. Drummond should be directed by that Court to quit the Country, or in the event of your not receiving any communication from Mr. Drummond within Forty-eight hours from the time of the said letter having been delivered to him (provided the weather should not be such as to preclude any intercourse with His Majesty's Fleet) you are in either of these suppositions to proceed to vigorous hostilities, and use your utmost endeavours to accomplish the object abovementioned, of destroying the

Arsenals and all the Shipping of Copenhagen; and as far as may be consistent with this operation to capture or destroy the Trade of Shipping of the Danes, Swedes or Russians within the Baltic, and to annoy and distress them in such other manner as may be in your Power, according to the rights and usages of War. As soon as the final determination of the Court of Denmark shall be known to you, you are to send off a fast sailing vessel with intelligence thereof to our Secretary for our information; and if contrary to His Majesty's wishes, that Court should be so ill-advised as to risk all the consequences of War, you are in such case to send another with an account of your operations against Copenhagen, as soon as you shall have been able to ascertain the degree of success with which they have been attended; and as in either of the cases forementioned further operations will remain to be carried on within the Baltic, You are to continue with the Fleet under your command within the Sound until you shall receive from us such Orders as the situation of affairs may then appear to require; As it will probably be impossible to carry into execution the eventual Instructions herein contained for destroying the Arsenals. And whereas it is our intention that Admiral Dickenson should remain at Yarmouth for the purpose of carrying on the public Service there, and to watch the motions of the Enemy's ships now in the different Ports of Holland, you are previously to your leaving Yarmouth Roads furnish him with such Orders and Instructions as you may conceive it to be necessary for his guidance, according to the intelligence he may from time to time receive of the state of the Enemy, and to acquaint our Secretary of his proceedings for his information. Given, &c, &c, 4th. March, 1801. Sir Hyde Parker, Admiral of the Blue.

(1) George III
(2) League of Armed Neutrality
(3) Secretary of State for War and the Colonies
(4) Secretary of State for Foreign Affairs.
(5) Nicholas Vansittart, later 1st. Baron Bexley, sent by Lord Hawkesley on special mission to Denmark, February, 1801, to make clear England's position. He left Copenhagen on 16 March, 1801.

The North Sea squadrons duly sailed, and, the embassy to Copenhagen having failed to convince the Crown Prince of the British case, on 1 April attacked the heavily fortified port. It was, of course, at this battle that Nelson put his telescope to his blind eye. The battle concluded, in the main, successfully for Britain, with the Danish Fleet effectively destroyed. Alas, it was an unnecessary expenditure of life.

Top Right: A top-sail schooner at Whitby. (FMS)

Bottom Right: Scarborough, an ancient borough, was a dependent port of Hull, as was Bridlington. Here vessels of various sizes sit in the Harbour. (FMS)

CHAPTER 11

On 24 March Paul I was assassinated, leaving his son, Alexander I, to succeed. There was a Palace Revolution, of which, it is thought, his heir was well aware, though not of its ultimate outcome.

Thomas became aware of the Tsar's death:

Sunday [March] *29th. This Morning an express arrived at this Town that the Emperor of Russia was dead but this is not asserted yet for truth, as we expect to hear further concerning the Above Affair in a short time.*

In due course the new Tsar was proclaimed, though not crowned until the following October:

Tuesday [April] *7th 1801 This Night there was an Illumination at this Town, in honour to the New Emperor's Coronation, in some windows there was two Candles and some only one, such (deletion) an Illumination was never seen before by an Englishman.*

In 1990, for the first time for a great many years, the people of Estonia marked Christmas by just such an illumination of a candle in each window. For Thomas it was a delight. Thomas' enchantment by this illumination is salutary, for we who are accustomed to well-lit streets, and houses lit by electricity, have no concept of the darkness that must have prevailed in the night in a town in 1801, so that the simple act of lighting every window, even with only one candle, would seem magical to the homesick crews.

One month later Alexander renounced the claim to Malta. Then, faced with, among other things, Nelson and the Baltic Fleet apparently threatening Reval, called off the embargo in May. There had, of course, been intense diplomatic activity, which Nelson's action might have spoilt, and normal diplomatic relations, with all manner of provisos, were restored in the person of Lord St. Helens as Ambassador and Plenipotentiary. His and his Chargé d'Affaires' correspondence survives. Lord St Helens was permitted by His Majesty's Government to make some small concessions: only Royal Naval ships were to stop and search the ships of the Baltic States; privateers must let them pass.

He was, however, enjoined by the Foreign Office to send to England a constant stream of information about every conceivable aspect of Russian trade, social and political life, in the brand new ciphers with which he was furnished. Mr Benjamin Garlike, Chargé d'Affaires, was forced to ask Nelson to withdraw his somewhat threatening presence lest he disturb the delicate balance of negotiations. With the lifting of the embargo came the freeing of the prisoners, and a flurry of letters from the restored Stephen Shairp and his brother record the arrangements they made to expedite the relief. To save time, horses were hired for the most distant men to ride. The need for ship-building materials was by then even more desperate because of the loss of the final cargoes of the previous year, and because the Government had heeded Stephen Shairp's advice and had refused to allow the Russia Company to trade through neutral ports. This form of conveyance may have seemed a mixed blessing to men as little used to riding as they were to walking, but the image conjured up of this shabby band trotting seawards on their native ponies gives a little light relief. Certainly Thomas Etty's account of his return, hitching lifts on carts and a raft, is quite light-hearted.

Sunday 10th 1801 This Day [erasure] *to our Great satisfaction received Orders to make ready for Marching down to Riga as soon as we could get Waggons and horses*

Monday 11th. 1801
This Day Received 60 Copeaks also Received Orders to make ready for Marching on next Wednesday
[Page 32]
Morning towards Riga, in hope of once more returning to Old England in our own Ships.
Tuesday 12th 1801 Made all preparations for marching next Morning
Wednesday 13th 1801 About 10 O Clock this Morning proceeded on our Journey towards Riga, This stage travelled 25 Werse,

The daily stages were much longer on the return journeys; on 6 June Stephen Shairp, now restored to his duties in St Petersburg, wrote to Mr. Evan Nepean, Secretary to the Admiralty, to assure him that he had authorised allowances for 'horsehire' to expedite the re-manning of the ships and to hasten the delivery of the precious raw materials to naval shipyards.

Thursday 14th May 1801 Early this Morning proceeded on our Journey passed through a very thick wood 6 Werses Long - very hot weather. towards the Evening thick Cloudy weather with
[Page 33]
Thunder and lighting attended with showers of Rain. This stage travelled 28 Werses
Friday 15th May 1801 About 3 OClock this Morning Arose and proceeded forward Cloudy with Showers of Rain This stage went 37 Werse
Saturday 16th May 1801 About 4 OClock this Morning Arose and proceeded on towards Riga About 7 OClock came to a Town called Wolmer, but the

Waggons and the Caravans was left behind about 10 Werses on account of the horses being turned out to feed last Night and this Morning the three horses belonging to Caravan which the Captains

[Page 34]

rode in could not be found which detain'd us very much but after a little time the horses was found and the Caravan came to Town After having renewed our Stock of Provisions about a eleven OClock we proceed forward this stage 37 Verse

The frantic searching for the Captains' horses would have led to ill-tempered impatience, but the division still managed 37 'werses' that day, a formidable total after a late start.

Sunday Morning 17th May This Morning past through a small Village met with a light Caravan got up and rode 15 Werse This Night cross'd a River upon a floating bridge at 10 P.M. came to a house 22 Werse from Riga were we slept all Night in a hayloft. This stage we came 62 Werse

[Page 35]

Monday 18th 1801 Early this Morning arose and proceeded on towards Riga About Eleven oClock arrived in the Town This Stage 22 Werse

Tuesday 19th 1801 This Morning Early the Baggage arrived in the Town and we was Quarter'd at a house without the Wall all our ships Company was put into two small Rooms.

Wednesday 20th May, 1801

Thursday 21st May. This Day Received 70 Stivers for 1 Week

Friday 22nd May 1801 -Sunday 24th May [date only]

[Page 36]

Monday 25th 1801 Received 84 Stivers

Tuesday 26th 1801 Made a settlement with Mr. Coverdale. Received 70 Stivers Balance money

Captain Coverdale's rôle as banker had ended, but there is little doubt that his careful husbanding of their precious resource would have protected the men from the worst starvation. The true extent of the Masters' anxieties seems to have been unrecorded, at least publicly. Captain Cramp had stated in March in an oblique reference in a letter that censorship was in place; others cautiously said that they would describe their situation in more detail when they returned home.

Wednesday 27th 1801

Thursday 28th May This Day received Orders from our Captain to go down to Bulderoye, to be ready to go on board the Ship on Friday Morning

Friday 29th May 1801 This Morning Our Captain took Possession of the Ship George.

Contrary to all Thomas' fears, the *George* was still there at Bulroye Quay. So, probably, were most of the others. The icing-up of the Gulf would have seen to that.

Trade was resumed, but many lessons had been learned, and there was never again quite the same dependence on the Baltic for supplies of timber and hemp. The new colonies were found to offer good sources, and trade gradually diversified. A further episode in 1807-8, when Alexander in turn wavered in his alliance, brought further concern. Ironically, however, it was to be the same experience, the long march through the Russian winter, which began the decline of Napoleon's career, in the Retreat from Moscow.

Not all the timber went for Naval purposes, and much of it went to build boats as well as ships. This is a selection of boats of all sizes at Whitby. (FMS)

CHAPTER 12

Thomas Etty was only 20 when he kept the Journal for the *George*. One of the initial and most important pieces of information it gives is that the Journal itself was kept in response to the Emperor's orders. Merchant seamen ashore were not normally subject to ship's discipline, and therefore, at least in theory, would have had to be strongly guarded. Thomas Coverdale discharged his crew officially when they were taken from the ship, to avoid paying the Seamen's Sixpence. Other Whitby musters show the same action. Guarding the crews would have been expensive for the Russians, so a ship's log was demanded to signify that the crew was 'under command'. Captain Coverdale was expected to command his crew and to act as their paymaster. The message was reinforced as soon as the crew reached its destination by the stoppage of pay. Thereafter, the guard marched back to Riga and the crews were left to cope. There must, therefore, have been some 200 logs, roughly one for each ship, though some of the smaller ships' crews might have been amalgamated. As far as is known, only Thomas' log has survived.

Hull, with a population of some 22,000, had the second highest number of ships trapped in Russia, some 27, as well as others from its dependent ports like Bridlington and Scarborough. The number of Whitby seamen captured is unknown, but most of the 45 vessels were large, brigs and ships, carrying crews of some 14 or 15. There were some, like the *Thaïs*, with fewer recorded, but there was probably a loss of at least 600 men and boys, at least three quarters of whom would be breadwinners. There was serious distress among seamen's families. In Hull the Hull Marine Society paid 10s 6d per week to all the families involved, and the Mayor's appeal raised well over £1,300. The charity performance in the theatre of *Jane Shore* raised £26.3s, augmented by a two-guinea donation from a concerned citizen. In Whitby the Shipowners' Society raised their own relief fund, responding with patient benevolence to irate letters from the Russia Company requesting contributions to the official fund. They capitulated, faced with evidence that the Company was actually supporting Whitby wives. Other ports would have made similar efforts, and in smaller places the burden would fall on the Overseers of the Poor, already hard-pressed by war conditions. But the worst would be the uncertainty as to whether the men and boys would return. Those families who knew the Master to be a fair-minded man might feel some confidence, but for many there must have been only a prolonged and sickening fear. For some of both men and boys, of course, there was no one to care, for often boys were orphans, sent to sea by the Overseers. One wonders what their survival rate was.

Thomas, articulate, literate, of a family of the 'middling sort', eventually to become a small merchant himself, survived, and recorded with a light heart his return to Riga, at a far greater speed that on the outward journey. What happened to the demands of Zuckerbecker and Trompowski was not recorded. Suffice to say that the crews loaded the ships and eventually sailed for 'Old England', as Thomas in a moment of patriotic fervour called it. The voyage of the *George* eventually ended over a year after the embargo began, and 20 months after the voyage had started. It ended in the Thames, and William Langborne laconically paid the Seamen's Sixpence for the *George* at Whitby Seamen's Hospital on 24 November, 1801.

But he did not pay for Thomas Etty, or for the man Christiansen, whose wife's desperate appeal was quoted by the Russia Company to Thomas Robinson, Deputy Collector of Customs at Whitby. Why was Thomas Etty the keeper of the *George's* Journal? Were William Langborne and Thomas Coverdale conspiring just a little over Seamen's Sixpence? Were they docking just a little less from each man's pay and omitting seamen's names from the muster? Given that Whitby Hospital was a beneficiary of the scheme and that without it the Owners would have been faced with far higher parish poor rates for the relief of distressed seamen and their families, that seems unlikely.

Were they understating the numbers of the crew recorded on the muster to delude the hated Impress service into thinking they were already undermanned, should they fall into company with a 'press tender' on the homeward trip? The Navy could legally press seamen from inward-bound ships, though they were not supposed to leave them unable to man the ship safely. Or was Thomas a stray from another Whitby ship, absorbed into Thomas Coverdale's crew because he was known to the Master, and given the Journal to write by way of keeping him in order, or because he was more literate than any other seaman? One of the Mates had, after all, been left behind to guard the ships. Was it Thomas Coverdale who docked Thomas' pay to curb his high spirits? Or was he simply passing on the instructions from the Russians? Siberia was a dreaded possibility, and the people of the *George* had been to some extent lucky in their place of imprisonment. Some crews marched for two months and buried their dead by the roadside as they fell.

Thomas kept his Journal, right to the end at Riga, and he kept it to pass to his children. Because he did so it has survived. Were the others collected up by the Russians, or were they thrown away by jubilant seamen? Are there others hidden away in private hands?

The wind-eroded gravestone of John Lott's widow in Whitby parish churchyard. It is quite probable that John Lott, who became a Master himself, died at sea, as did at least one third of all Masters. (RB)

The gravestone of Jeremiah Robinson, Francis Gibson's predecessor as Comptroller of Customs, agent for many years for the Russia Company. His son Thomas, also commemorated on this stone, succeeded him as agent, and was Deputy Customer. It was he who coped with the battle between the Shipowners Society and the Company. (RB)

This leaning memorial may be the grave of John Nicholson of the George; the other possibility, mentioned in the text, is his father. The list of names on the stone shows clearly the experience of so many Whitby families, buried afar, but commemorated at home. (RB)

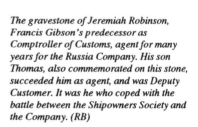

CHAPTER 13

The chance discovery of the Journal of Thomas Etty inevitably induced considerable curiosity about the author, and at the start of the search for Thomas' identity, the Journal was the only clue. The only 'Etty' routinely mentioned in reference books is William Etty, R.A., the early 19th-century York artist, 1787-1842. A search of the will indexes at the Borthwick Institute for Historical Research at York revealed several Etty wills, but of Thomas Etty, mariner, there was no sign. It was initially his absence from the ship's muster roll which was disconcerting, though that is less surprising in the light of other absences. The only clue the Journal contained was the note at the end of the book that it had been handed over in Hull in 1874. However, there is a remarkable series of trade directories for Hull, beginning at the end of the 18th century, and a search of these revealed that there was indeed a Thomas Etty in Hull listed in every directory between 1806 and 1851 as Thomas Etty, wholesale confectioner, and once also as a gingerbread maker, of Church Lane. He appeared in the Burgess Rolls of the same town from 1832 until 1854-55. The *Hull Advertiser* recorded him as having died in Church Lane on 30 May, 1854, aged 74. There seemed little to connect the keeper of the ship's Journal with a confectioner (or gingerbread maker), save that Thomas' log provided an unwitting piece of evidence. When the Zuckerbecker incident had come to the notice of the crews while they were imprisoned, Thomas mentioned it, in some despair. Instead of accepting the name Zuckerbecker as a surname, which it was, Thomas translated it into 'a sugarmaker', implying either some knowledge of German, or, as it transpired, of the confectionery trade. The indexes to the obituary notices in the *Hull Advertiser* produced several references to wives of 'Mr. Thomas Etty', who seems to have had four wives, one of whom outlived him. More revealing still was the obituary notice for Mrs. Esther Etty, who died at her son's in Hull, at an advanced age, in 1829, and who was described in the obituary notice as the mother of William Etty, R.A..

Alexander Gilchrist's *Life of William Etty* revealed that this was indeed so, and that Thomas Etty was William's elder brother, who, as a sailor in a whaling ship on leave about 1798, had given William, then a printer's apprentice in Hull, a box of water-colour paints. The same book gave the home of their father, Matthew, a miller, as being Feasegate in York, of the parish of All Saints, Pavement, (with Little Saint Peter's, in which Feasegate was actually situated). The baptismal register for All Saints' and St. Peter's is missing for a large part of the late 18th century, but the Bishop's Transcripts are good, and they revealed that Thomas Etty was born to Matthew Etty, and Esther his wife, on 9 April, 1780, and baptised on the 15th. William, described as the '7th. son' of Matthew and Esther, was born and baptised on 10 March, 1787, so would have been an 11-year-old when Thomas gave him the box of paints. It is a gesture which accords with the amused humanity with which Thomas, then aged 20, records the march to Fellin in December, 1800, and life in a large family would make acceptance of the cramped conditions aboard a ship, and in the worst of his imprisonment, easier to bear.

It has been possible to assemble quite a large file on Thomas. The Etty family, most of whose present members now live in the Netherlands, after having established themselves during Thomas' lifetime in the Dutch East Indies in the sugar trade, were very close and supportive of each other. The five boys of Thomas' generation kept in touch with each other, though they were rarely able to meet as a group, and those who were successful supported those who were not. William, the youngest, inestimably gifted but hopelessly impractical, was protected from hardship by his brother Walter, and from the practicalities of life by a devoted niece, Betsey. In his turn, when he was wealthy and successful, he kept in touch with Thomas, who seems from letters to have been less successful, but soft-hearted and susceptible. His parents, Matthew and Esther, appear to have set Thomas up in the family trade of confectionery in Hull when he married his first wife, Elizabeth, but a letter from his younger brother, Charles, a sea-captain in the East Indies trade, to Betsey refers to Thomas' 'bad wife', presumably Jane, his second wife, but possibly Mary, his third, and wishes he would leave her, and take his children out east. She must have been very bad indeed for such a suggestion to be made in the early 19th century. Certainly Mrs. Esther Etty forgave all her son Thomas' debts in her will, but carefully left the house he occupied to her eldest son, Walter. Thomas had been apprenticed to sea in Whitby at the age of 13. Why he left the sea is unknown, and how he escaped the 'press' in a seaport like Hull during the Napoleonic Wars is a mystery. He must somehow have gained exemption, possibly by providing an exchange.

William painted him in 1811, visited him, and took him to Beverley for picnic treats on the Westwood. His parents lived with him from time to time, and his son, Charles, to whom the Journal was given, joined his Uncle Charles in Java, marrying Suki, daughter of Charles senior. The grandson, Matthew, an engineer, to whom the Journal was given, died a year later in Hull of 'brain-fever'. Thus the Journal must have left the family. The portrait of Thomas is in the Netherlands, in the care of Thomas Etty, collateral descendant of Thomas of the Journal.

Thomas had several children, including the two daughters who were living with him at the time of the 1841 census. He lived in Church Lane, a street in the Old Town which ran from Holy Trinity Church down to the River Hull. The staith is the only part of Church Lane to have survived the bombing of Hull in

1941. He was at times a Methodist, but some of his children were baptised at Holy Trinity. His brother William wavered on the brink of Catholicism, lured by the imagery of the mediaeval Minsters, York and Beverley, that he loved.

Thomas' neat sloping hand continued through his life, and his kindly nature is evident. The hardships of housekeeping on too little seem to have dogged him all his life, though he was a freeman of York by inheritance, and an elector of Hull under the 1832 Reform Act. Yet this ordinary man has given us the only sustained insight into such an extraordinary event.

There are other people who stand out from these events: there is Thomas Coverdale, Master of the *George*, whose will of 1823 suggests that he was a bachelor. He was a close friend of the owner, William Langborne, and one of three brothers who were all successful Whitby Masters. Another member of the family, Norrison Coverdale, living in London, owned a Whitby-built East Indiaman called the *Coverdale*, whose log of two trips to India is held in the archives of the Honourable East India Company. There are the agents such as Mr. Moore, who travelled with the groups of seamen to act as interpreters; the masters who wrote letters home, carefully worded to warn, but also to reduce alarm; provincial journalists like Mr. Peck, the editor of the *Hull Packet*, to whom William Etty was apprenticed as a printer, and who took up with righteous fury the cause of the provincial merchants who stood to lose everything, and of the wives and children of the imprisoned men; Mr. Forster, the President of the Russia Company, trying to make the Government see the problems of his fellow merchants 'that side the water', while understanding the political implications. Evan Nepean, Secretary to the Admiralty, juggled demands for help with resources stretched to the limit by global war.

In the background were the unknown citizens who contributed to the Lord Mayor of London's appeal for the families of the seamen, at a time of national stress, and of desperate strains on the system of poor relief. The advertisements for the appeal are juxtaposed with complex schemes for soup kitchens for feeding the growing army of poor. There were the members of the Marine Society of Hull, the second-worst hit town, who were prepared to pay out 10s 6d to every family every week until the crisis was over, an open-ended commitment which must have meant facing an seemingly never-ending round of fund-raising. Shadowy figures were the women who waited at home, deprived of a regular income, anxious about the lack of news, or, having received a precious letter, willing to share it, through the provincial press, for the sake of others less fortunate. There were some women like Catherine Kneeshaw, wife of the master of the *Harpooner*, of Whitby, who in desperation took on the seemingly mighty Russia Company to obtain help and money. She was awarded £3.19.0. Twelve Whitby women in all asked the Company for help, as far as is known, and the disbursements, on a sliding scale, probably represented their rank rather than their needs! Others would simply ask the Overseers, or the owners of the ships, who were themselves somewhat pressed.

Still alive at this time was Mrs. Margaret Campion, Freeman of the Russia Company, and founder with her sons of one of the Whitby banks. Her family's shipping and banking interests must have been heavily involved. Indeed, *Campion* was one of the captured Whitby ships.

Lieutenant Norris sailed on the thankless cartel run to Russia, where he met a hostile welcome, arranged by the Tsar's propagandists, which almost led to a lynching of his crew for ill-treatment of his passengers. The Russian soldiers who were his passengers themselves rescued the situation by rushing ashore to reassure the angry mob that they had not been ill-treated. Yet Norris, far from leaving in haste, took time to serve his country with the espionage which would have greatly encouraged the Government. Benjamin Garlike, Chargé d'Affaires after the death of Paul, laboured to conduct the delicate negotiations to re-establish diplomatic relations, while securing the release of the prisoners, and hoping that the rattling of Nelson's cutlasses would not spoil all his work. Pervading the atmosphere was the mad Tsar Paul himself, haunting the whole affair with his obsessions and fears, and the summary brutalities which led in the end to the palace coup which ended his life.

'This side the water', in Whitby, there was Thomas Robinson, Deputy Collector of Customs, in his room at the Seamen's Hospital, from which much seafaring business was conducted. He mediated between the powerful Russia Company, which wanted him to contribute Whitby's collection to the total fund, and the independent-minded shipowners and merchants of the town who wished to look after their own. Theirs was after all the greatest burden borne by any town, and it is perhaps just that the only Journal should survive from the town which contributed more ships to the Baltic trade and suffered greater human distress from these events than any other port in Great Britain. Yet, curiously, no whisper of the event remained in Whitby's consciousness until Thomas' Journal appeared. This had been just another difficulty to be endured in a town used to absent men, loss at sea, war, privateering, imprisonment and poverty; except that Lewis Carroll was an enthusiast for Whitby, where he spent holidays. The beach is thought to have inspired *The Walrus and the Carpenter*. Did folk memory of a mad Emperor inspire the Red Queen?

Above all the official figures who pervade the documents about the Baltic Incident two stand out; Stephen Shairp, H.M. Consul-General, and Alexander Shairp, his brother and Vice-Consul. Stephen set out on a difficult fact-finding mission in a lugger and post-chaises, all the way to St. Petersburg and back in vain in the late autumn weather. Rebuffed, he set about that which he knew best, political analysis of his second country, Russia, writing masterly reports and analyses of trade and court politics, advising the government not to panic under pressure from the Russia Company, of which his firm, Walter Shairp and Son, was a member, and corresponding through neutral countries with his brother and his contacts. He was indefatigable, and returned in triumph as Consul-General when all was resolved.

His brother, Alexander, whose letters, in a smaller, rounder, less commanding hand, also survive, remained in Russia, and through his actions in setting up relief networks for distributing money and organising the raising of that money by the hard-pressed Russia Company Merchants, already punitively fined, enabled Thomas Etty and all the others to receive little handouts from the Merchants which probably meant the survival of many more than might have been expected. There is an extant letter from Alexander, in which he described his emotions at the quayside at Cronstadt as he watched these poor seamen marched off to what he, with deeper understanding than they would have of Russian inefficiency, could only see as death by the roadside. His organising skill and personal generosity in purchasing for each man caught at Cronstadt a sheepskin coat, hat, gloves, boots and two pairs of socks, spared at least those the barefoot horrors felt by Captain Ward's crew marching from Riga. That he was reimbursed was irrelevant; he had no idea at the time whether he would be; and even then he made the desperate winter journey back to England, presumably through neutral countries, to report in person to his brother and the Government. This is a book of unlikely heroes, unsung, laconic, unglamorous. It is a book about endurance by ordinary people of the events imposed upon them by politics, vanity and ambition, but it is also a book about the better side of government, in which men like Pitt and Canning, and their successors and public servants, can take up the cause of ordinary men. It is about the funny side, of men who refused to march in step to please their captors, and laughed at the difficulties of trying to sleep 200 to two small rooms, and who hitched lifts to freedom on river rafts. We owe a debt to Thomas Etty, mariner of Whitby, freeman of York and confectioner of Hull, for bringing this to light.

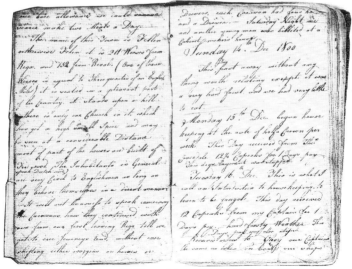

The Description of Fellin, and the problems of frugality. (IP)

THOMAS ETTY'S SUBSISTENCE IN RUSSIA.

Thomas himself explained that 1 Rouble = 100 Copeaks. He gave an exchange rate of 8 Roubles to £1 English. As a regular seaman he would have a shrewd idea about exchange rates. His allotment from the Emperor and from the Merchants' fund came to 2852½ Copeaks, and he was forced to borrow a further 200 from Captain Coverdale.

Between his arrival at Fellin and his arrival back at Riga he existed on this small sum for 157 days, at an average rate of 19½ Copeaks per day, though often less. If 100 Roubles was equal to 30 old pence, then 1 old penny was equal to approximately 3½ Copeaks. Thomas was therefore existing on an average of approximately 5½d per day. The only price he gave is of beef at 5 Copeaks a pound, or about 1½d, and that would have included bone, fat and gristle. He commented that bread was very dear, as were other items, so it is unlikely that his 5½d. [about 2p] would offer anything above bare subsistence. Had he been working in England at that time, then his daily wage even as a labourer would have been about three times as much. Stivers, which Thomas received on his return to Riga, were small coins; the word seems to have been applied to the smaller coins in many northern European currencies.

THOMAS ETTY'S JOURNAL

The Journal is kept in a small book bound in the hand-sewn rough hessian which was often used for the ship-board covers of log-books. These books would then be re-bound by the owners before storing. The paper is quite fine, unlike the sometimes very coarse paper of working logs. It is laid and water-marked. The ink is iron-galls, and the paper is slightly foxed, and parts of some of the edges are damaged.

This is a transcript of the Journal as Thomas Etty wrote it, with the contractions expanded and the erasures omitted. Those days on which only the date or the weather were given have been grouped. Text which has been lost because of damage is shown by three dots, ... These are the sections which have not been used in the text. The gaps are indicated by the ~~~~~~.

The Journal

[Title page]
[Very faint figures, probably days in a series of months, as on last page].
December 1   December   The Confinement in Russia December 1st 1800
[The above are very faint, and rather like doodles, or false starts. Attempts may even have been made to erase them].~~~~~~

[Page 7] [Page damaged] in the Morning being the 5th December proceeded on our Journey under the same guard of Soldiers,
Friday 5th proceeded on our Journey as Usual.
Saturday 6th December shifted our Baggage waggons and horses proceeded on our Journey as before.
[Page 8] [Page damaged]...aggons as before proceeded on our...urney under the same guard of Soldier as before.~~~~~~

Monday 8th December, so this piece of business being concluded we proceed on our Journey along with our waggons and Soldiers as usual. Night coming on we stop'd at the next house at we came to were we staid all night slept upon straw, but not much rest was to be had by reason of so many
[Page 13] people being confined in so small a Compass.~~~~~~

Friday 12th Was called out very early in Morning to shift our baggage waggons and horses and to prepare for Marching. About 6 O'Clock set out on our Intended Journey Guarded with the same Company of Soldiers as before, passed through several thick gloomy Woods which continued for the space of 7 or 8 Werses The Frost set in, the Roads begun to grow hard all which was very great in our Favour in respect to travelling. About Eleven O'Clock in the Forenoon got sight of our place of Destination, or the Town were we was appointed to be quarter'd at. continueing to freeze very hard.~~~~~~

Friday 19th December 1800. This being some saint Day or other, there was no beef to be got, this was not to our satisfaction in the least as our appetites was very keen. More Moderate rather inclined to Thaw. Cloudy weather.

Saturday 20th December 1800 Fine serene weather attended with
[Page 19]
Light breezes of wind. &c.

Sunday 21st December 1800
Strong gales of wind from the Northard & Eastward with Cold frosty weather. Towards the Evening heavy Gales with much snow and Sleet.

Monday 22nd December 1800 More Moderate Milde and Soft Weather with a little Snow.

Tuesday 23nd December 1800 Fine serene weather. This Day received 105 Copeaks to serve me 6 Days, This was 5 Copeaks more allowance than we got before

Wednesday 24th December 1800 This Day fine soft weather Inclinable to Thaw. Strong Breezes of wind towards the Evening.~~~~~~

Friday 26th December 1800 Thick foggy weather with light Airs of wind. Strong Breezes of wind towards the Evening &c.~~~~~~

[Page 21
Sunday Dec/ember 28th 1800 Sharp Frosty Weather with cold winds and a little Snow.

Monday December 29th 1800 Hard Frosty weather with cold strong winds. This morning received 135 Copeaks from Mr. Coverdale to serve me till next Monday morning.

Tuesday December 30th 1800 Thick Cloudy weather attended with snow.

Wednesday December 31st 1800 Hard Frosty weather. This being the Last Day in the Old Year towards the Evenging snowy Weather.

Thursday January 1st 1801 This being the first Day of the new year fine clear Sun shiney weather &c Under command still.

[Page 22]

Friday January 2nd 1801 Hard Frosty weather Thick and Cloudy, with stormy winds and much Snow towards the Evening, &c.~~~~~~

Sunday January 4th 1801 Thick Cloudy weather Inclinable to Thaw, strong Breezes towards the Evening

Monday January 5th 1801 This Day received from Captain Coverdale 106 Copeaks to serve me till Tuesday the 13th.January.

[Page 23]

Tuesday January 6th 1801 Thick and Cloudy with strong Gales of Wind and Sleet.

Wednesday January 7th 1801 [*altered from 1800*] Strong Breezes of wind with cloudy weather Ditto Wr and Frosty towards the Evening. this Day was also kept the same as Yesterday.

Thursday January 8th 1801 Hard Frosty and Clear weather with light Breezes of wind.

Friday January 9th 1801 Frosty but Clear weather with strong Breezes of wind

Saturday January 10th 1801 Thick foggy weather &c.

[Page 24]

Sunday January 11th 1801 Frosty but Cloudy weather, Under command of our Captains still the same as when on board of our respective Ships by an order &c.

Monday January 12th 1801 Frosty weather with a little Snow in the Morning &c.

Tuesday January 13th 1801 This Day received from Mr. Coverdale 50 Copeaks or half a Ruble.

Wednesday January 14th 1801 This Day received from Mr. Coverdale 85 Copeaks, This and the above fifty that I received Yesterday is to serve me till Tuesday next.

Thursday January 15th 1801 Thick cloudy weather with a little Sleet towards the Evening &c.

[Page 25]

Friday January 16th 1801 to Monday January 19th 1801 weather or date

Tuesday January 20 1801 Received from Mr. Coverdale 35 Capeaks

Wednesday January 21st 1801 Received from Mr. Coverdale 1 Ruble This and the above 35 is to serve me till Wednesday next

Thursday January 22nd 1801 This Day received from Mr. Coverdale 2 Rubles and 45 Capeaks. This was the Overplus Money That was sent from the Merchants.

[Page 26]

Friday January 23rd 1801 to Tuesday January 27th weather and date

Wednesday January 28th Ditto Weather This Day received 35 Capeaks

Thursday January 29th 1801 Received 135 Capeaks

Friday January 30th 1801 to Monday February 2nd weather and date

Tuesday February 3rd 1801 Wednesday February 4th received from Mr. Coverdale 35 Capeaks

Thursday February 5th to Thursday 12. 1801 date only

[Page 27]

Friday February 13th 1801 Received 70 Capeaks. Merchants Allowance

Saturday February 14th to Tuesday 17th February date only

Wednesday 18th February 1801. Received 50 Capeaks from Mr. Coverdale. Money lent.

Thursday 19th 1801. Received 50 Capeaks

Friday 20th 1801 Snowy weather

Saturday 21st 1801 Received from Mr. Coverdale 170 Capeaks to serve me till next Saturday

Sunday 22nd 1801 to Friday 27th date only

Saturday 28th Received 70 Capeaks. Merchants Money~~~~~~~

[Page 28]

Sunday 15th [March] 1801 to Friday 20th 1801 date only

Saturday March 21st. 1801

[Page 29]

Received 50 Copeaks Lent and 70 Capeaks Merchants Money

Sunday 22nd Friday to 27th date only

Saturday 28th Received 70 Capeakes

Monday 30th. 1801. Tuesday 31st. Received 1 Ruble and 50 Copeaks Emperors allowance

Wednesday April 1st 1801 to Saturday 4th 1801 date only

[Page 30]

Sunday 5th 1801 This being Easter Sunday Received 30 Copeaks. Merchants Money for the Month of February

Monday April 6 1801

Wednesday 8th to Sunday 12 April 1801 date only

Monday 13th 1801 Received 70 Copeaks Merchants Allowance

Tuesday 14th to Thursday 16th date only

Friday 17 Received 50 Copeaks Money Lent

Saturday 18; Sunday 19

Monday 20th April 1801 Received 70 Copeaks

Tuesday 21nd April 1801 to Thursday 23rd date only

Friday 24th: Received 50 Capeaks Money Lent.

Saturday 25th Sunday 26th

Monday 27th Received 1 Ruble(large scrawl!)

Tuesday 28th to

[Page 31]

Friday May 1st 1801 date only
Saturday May 2nd 1801 Received 1 Ruble
Sunday May 3rd to Tuesday May 5 date only
Wednesday 6th Received 80 Copeaks to serve till next Monday,
Thursday 7th to Saturday 9th 1801 date only~~~~~~

[*Change of hand*:] This Memorandum book was given to ''Matthew Etty'' by his Father in remembrance of his, Matthew Etty's ''Grandfather's'' confinement in Russia in 1800-1
Hull, January ...1874 (sgd) Chas. Etty

A TABLE of GREENWICH-HOSPITAL DUTY, calculated from 1 MONTH to 30 MONTHS, at 6d. per Month.

Months	Odd Days							Months	Odd Days						
	1 and 2,	3, 4, 5, 6, and 7,	8, 9, 10, 11, & 12,	13 to 17,	19 to 22,	23 to 27,	28, 29, 30, & 31.		1 and 2,	3, 4, 5, 6, and 7,	8, 9, 10, 11, & 12,	13 to 17,	18 to 22,	23 to 27,	28, 29, 30, & 31.
	s. d.	s. d.	s. d.	s. d.	s. d.	s. d.	s. d.		s. d.	s. d.	s. d.	s. d.	s. d.	s. d.	s. d.
1	0 6	0 7	0 8	0 9	0 10	0 11	1 0	16	8 0	8 1	8 2	8 3	8 4	8 5	8 6
2	1 0	1 1	1 2	1 3	1 4	1 5	1 6	17	8 6	8 7	8 8	8 9	8 10	8 11	9 0
3	1 6	1 7	1 8	1 9	1 10	1 11	2 0	18	9 0	9 1	9 2	9 3	9 4	9 5	9 6
4	2 0	2 1	2 2	2 3	2 4	2 5	2 6	19	9 6	9 7	9 8	9 9	9 10	9 11	10 0
5	2 6	2 7	2 8	2 9	2 10	2 11	3 0	20	10 0	10 1	10 2	10 3	10 4	10 5	10 6
6	3 0	3 1	3 2	3 3	3 4	3 5	3 6	21	10 6	10 7	10 8	10 9	10 10	10 11	11 0
7	3 6	3 7	3 8	3 9	3 10	3 11	4 0	22	11 0	11 1	11 2	11 3	11 4	11 5	11 6
8	4 0	4 1	4 2	4 3	4 4	4 5	4 6	23	11 6	11 7	11 8	11 9	11 10	11 11	12 0
9	4 6	4 7	4 8	4 9	4 10	4 11	5 0	24	12 0	12 1	12 2	12 3	12 4	12 5	12 6
10	5 0	5 1	5 2	5 3	5 4	5 5	5 6	25	12 6	12 7	12 8	12 9	12 10	12 11	13 0
11	5 6	5 7	5 8	5 9	5 10	5 11	6 0	26	13 0	13 1	13 2	13 3	13 4	13 5	13 6
12	6 0	6 1	6 2	6 3	6 4	6 5	6 6	27	13 6	13 7	13 8	13 9	13 10	13 11	14 0
13	6 6	6 7	6 8	6 9	6 10	6 11	7 0	28	14 0	14 1	14 2	14 3	14 4	14 5	14 6
14	7 0	7 1	7 2	7 3	7 4	7 5	7 6	29	14 6	14 7	14 8	14 9	14 10	14 11	15 0
15	7 6	7 7	7 8	7 9	7 10	7 11	8 0	30	15 0	15 1	15 2	15 3	15 4	15 5	15 6

A TABLE of GREENWICH-HOSPITAL DUTY, calculated from 1 DAY to 1 MONTH, at 6d. per Month.

Number of Days.	Pence
31, 30, 29, 28	6
27, 26, 25, 24, 23	5
22, 21, 20, 19, 18	4
17, 16, 15, 14, 13	3
12, 11, 10, 9, 8	2
7, 6, 5, 4, 3	1
2, 1	0

A Whitby printer produced this useful ready reckoner for calculating the sixpences due after each period at sea. (WLP)

APPENDIX 3.

This is a list of some of the Russian towns to which the men marched; Imperial Russian names have been used. Some of them are so distorted by attempts to read the Cyrillic alphabet and then pronounce the Russian names that they are not yet identified!

Dorpat
Fellin (Viljandii)
Gdon
Jaroslavl
Lemsal
Moscow
Novgorod
Schwedsky
Smolensk
St Petersburg
Staraya Russia
Torjock
Tver
Velike Lugi
Voledema
Volokalamsk
Voronezh
Wasnavalchok
Wenden
Werro
Wolmar